First
Discussion
Starters

Speaking Fluency Activities for Lower-Level ESL/EFL Students

Keith S. Folse, Ph.D.

M.A. TESOL Program
University of Central Florida

Jeanine Ivone

English Language Institute
University of South Florida

Ann Arbor
THE UNIVERSITY OF MICHIGAN PRESS

To my many students over the years who asked me,
"How can I improve my speaking skills?" but
especially to those who made me think by insisting
that I give them an answer, which has resulted
in the Discussion Starters series.—KSF

To Nancy for a lifetime of patience and guidance,
and Freddy, my heart and soul.—JI

Acknowledgments

We would like to thank the teachers who were so helpful in the selection of some of the topics in this text as well as the field-testing of certain units. Their ideas, feedback, and support were extremely important in helping develop not only *First Discussion Starters* but also the whole Discussion Starters series.

We would also like to thank the many ESL/EFL professionals with whom we have been in touch electronically through TESL-L, TESLIE-L, and TESLMW-L.

Finally, we are particularly indebted to the great staff at the University of Michigan Press who are so supportive of our work, especially Kelly Sippell, Mary Erwin, Chris Milton, and Giles Brown.

Grateful acknowledgment is made to the following individuals, publishers, and journals for permission to reprint previously published materials.

The American Kennel Club for photograph of an Akita. Copyright © AKC, photo by Mary Bloom.

The Citadel for "Parade" photograph by Russell K. Pace from website.

John Grucelski for photograph of the Coliseum in Rome.

Pete Sickman-Garner for illustrations.

Contents

To the Teacher

Teaching Discussion Classes

Without a doubt, one of the most challenging teaching situations is a discussion or speaking class. In theory, the teacher (or a student) can bring up a given topic and the students will discuss its merits or controversial aspects. In reality, however, this is rarely the case. In most classes, the most confident students tend to dominate the discussion, and the weaker students, those who really need the class, quickly withdraw. In order to keep the "discussion" going, the teacher ends up trying to draw the students out. In effect, this "discussion" often becomes a question and answer exchange between the teacher and a few students.

In classes of students with lower levels of English proficiency, the difficulties associated with teaching a speaking class can be compounded when students' insufficient English language skills limit their ability to express their ideas in English. The teacher must then come up with activities that are interesting yet not beyond the linguistic capabilities of their students, a feat that is not at all easy. While many speaking books for lower-proficiency students have activities in which students talk about food preferences and favorite colors, these topics often lack the controversial or "discussable" aspect that a real discussion has. While students might indeed talk about their favorite colors, this is hardly a discussion. In a true discussion, speakers are pushed to ask the other participants why they hold a certain position. The activities in *First Discussion Starters* are an attempt to blend discussable topics for real discussions with L2 research on pair work (and group work) while taking into account the linguistic limitations and capabilities of lower-proficiency ESL/EFL learners.

With a wide variety of engaging topics and unique interactive exercises designed to keep the discussion flowing, *First Discussion Starters* aims to balance the speaking loads of all the students in the class and thus promote an environment in which everyone has not only a chance, but a real need, to speak out. In fact, many times the exercises have been designed so that the students cannot complete the speaking task unless everyone in the group participates and speaks up. Therefore, students actually need the input of other students to complete the discussion task. In addition to exercise design that encourages student interaction, we have taken care to choose topics that do not require large amounts of specialized vocabulary or complicated language. To be sure, some specialized language is needed for almost any discussion topic, whether it be court terms for a serious discussion of a court case or cooking terms for a lighter discussion of favorite childhood recipes.

Using the Book

The most important pedagogical point involved in using this book is that the teacher give the students the time and framework to think about their own ideas so they can form a coherent opinion. It is extremely important to realize that our students have a number of factors working against them: they may lack confidence in their English skills, they may not have any background information about the topic, they may not have participated much in group discussions, they may be not interested in the topic because they have not been engaged personally, and they may not have any opinion at all about the topic (though this last factor is definitely not limited to nonnative speakers). Because of the lower English level of most of the students using this book, it is therefore particularly important to allow the students extra time to prepare their ideas to identify key vocabulary or language structures needed to express a certain idea in a certain fashion.

These possible limitations of our students have been taken into account, and the exercises within each unit are set up in a special way in order to help the students develop and organize their ideas and thus foster confidence in their knowledge of the topic, which will facilitate speaking. Whenever a question for discussion is introduced, there is a prerequisite exercise that has the students write out their own ideas. This exercise sometimes consists of a series of short questions designed to guide the students through the critical thinking process. At other times, the exercise has two or three questions that are more general in nature but still aim to guide the students so that they can put down their ideas on paper.

This book is built on the premise that having to write out our thoughts on paper forces us to reexamine, rethink, and recycle our ideas until we have a much neater package. At workshops, when teachers are asked their opinion about a topic and then told, before everyone has had a chance to speak out, to write out their opinions in 25 to 50 words, it is usually the case that their written opinions have changed somewhat from their original opinions. Certainly the written opinions are more directed and more to the point. When teachers are then asked to continue talking about the topic in question, the discussion seems to flow much better. In addition, teachers who were reluctant to speak up before now do so. The printed word in front of them seems to be an anchor for those who were hesitant or reluctant to speak up before. The simple act of writing one's thoughts on paper before having to speak does make a real difference in not only the *quality* but also the *quantity* (fluency) of the discussion.

For example, when a student is suddenly confronted with the statement "People shouldn't drink and drive," it might be difficult for many students to say something that makes much sense and truly expresses their opinion. Most students in this situation in a group will be so nervous about what they are going to say that they can't and don't listen to the other students until after they themselves have spoken. Thus, what ensues more resembles a series of monologues than a dialogue or discussion of sorts. For this class to be a real learning and developing situation with interaction, it is much better—and we would argue necessary—to have the students write out their ideas briefly beforehand.

Topics for Discussion

A quick glance at the table of contents will reveal that the 24 units cover an extremely wide range of topics. Though most of the topics in the text are serious (censorship, cloning, and domestic violence), many others deal with lighter topics (proverbs, pets, and travel). The topics were chosen because they are of interest to our student base. In addition, topics that may become dated very quickly were not included.

Unlike other books on the market today, *First Discussion Starters* tries to avoid the use of imaginary situations for discussion (e.g., "Imagine that you were the president of the country. What would you do?"). When people have been challenged to come up with a potential solution to a task or problem, they rightfully expect to be able to hear what the "correct" answer is. For example, in the numerous court cases mentioned in this book, there is always a real court judgment given by a real judge or real jury or another official. After the students have discussed each other's verdicts and supporting reasons, they are then (and only then!) instructed to turn to the back of the book to discover the actual decision of the judge or the jury.

As often as possible, the activities, tasks, and topics chosen for this book are real situations from all over the world. When students are asked what they would do in a given situation, a real answer is provided.

Types of Interaction in the Exercises

Most of the units in this book introduce a problem or controversial topic at the beginning of the unit. This is then followed by a series of exercises designed to prepare all of the students so that they can express their ideas at the next class meeting. A unit usually includes several kinds of oral fluency activities, but some of the major types of activities are listed here.

Problem-solving tasks: A unique feature of this text is that *every* unit in this text has several tasks in which students must cooperate to solve a problem while using English.

Court cases: Exercises in Units 1, 6, 7, 10, 19, 20, 22. Each of these exercises pertains to a real court case that involves the topic of the unit. Students are told to work out their own solution as if they were the judge or jury or another authority with the power to decide the case and then discuss their ideas later in class. Actual decisions are revealed in the communication activities at the back of the book.

Finish the story: Units 8, 11. A story that has a unique ending has been begun in the unit, but the ending has deliberately been left off. Instructions are given for having students discuss possible endings and reasons for their choices. As with most of the material in this text, an actual story has been used.

Speaking puzzles: Units 4, 16. Students work in threes to complete a crossword puzzle. Each student has access to a unique set of some of the clues. Students must cooperate by giving spoken clues to each other so that they can complete the entire puzzle. Two students may have a clue for the same answer in the puzzle, but the clues have been written differently so as to foster discussion as to the meaning of each clue.

Role play: Units 2, 14, 19, 20, 21, 22, 23. Though the unit does not revolve around the role-play exercise, these units do include an exercise that has the students do some sort of role-play regarding the topic of the unit. Possible roles are often suggested, but it is up to the teacher to choose which roles should be used. Whether or not role plays succeed in class depends a lot on the dynamics of the given group of students.

Scales and questionnaires: Units 1, 2, 6, 9, 10, 12, 14, 17, 21, 24. Scales and questionnaires actively engage the students at a personal level; later on, students compare their responses with responses of other students in their groups.

Discussion and oral presentations: Units 5, 13. Though these units contain other types of interaction, one of the main points of these units is that students bring in related material from outside class to present to the rest of the class.

Put the story together: Units 3, 15, 18. Students work in large groups to solve a strip story. Each student has one piece of the story, and all students must work together or a solution is impossible.

Small group discussions: Units 1, 2, 3, 4, 5, 6, 7, 8, 9, 10, 11, 12, 13, 14, 15, 16, 17, 18, 19, 20, 21, 22, 23, 24. One of the main features of these units is an exercise that fosters active interaction among the members of a small group (three to five students).

Text Organization

First Discussion Starters consists of 24 self-contained units. There is ample background material in the text to start students on their way to a discussion. Teachers do not have to spend time searching for newspaper or magazine articles that most of the students in the class will be able to comprehend (which is in itself a major job for any teacher), and students do not have to do extensive outside reading in order to feel qualified to talk about the topics. Thus, students can spend their class time speaking about and discussing topics rather than reading them silently. (Naturally, teachers may assign additional readings to supplement the topics in *First Discussion Starters* if they wish.)

An important unique feature of this text is that there are efficient, that is, simple yet effective, homework exercises in which students must sort out their ideas and opinions before discussing or talking about the issues in the textbook. This allows all students to be prepared for the speaking activities in class and is of special importance to the weaker, less confident nonnative speakers. It also allows the teacher to feel confident that all the students in the class, regardless of their native country, education level, or age, now have a known common background about the topic. Some students will naturally know more about certain topics, but now the teacher at least has a common denominator from which to start discussion.

Each unit contains a number of exercises (usually around 8 to 10) that provide speaking preparation or speaking interaction about a central topic or idea. In most of these activities, students must work together in pairs or small groups to solve a problem, reach a consensus, discuss ideas, or complete some other kind of speaking task.

A particular strength of the design of this text is that there is no set pattern for introducing a topic. Units begin with a variety of presentations, including illustrations, questionnaires, court cases, and proverbs. This variety should keep a discussion course from becoming monotonous or too predictable after a few weeks.

Sequencing of Topics (units)

There is no one best way of sequencing the units or topics in this book. All units are independent of each other. Thus, the class could begin with any of the units and then continue with any other unit.

As much as possible, the difficulty level in the units is consistent. What is different, however, is the topic of the units. Thus, one of the few factors that might influence the "best" sequencing of units for a given group of students is the topics themselves. In general, students at this level will find the lighter topics toward the beginning of the book and the more serious topics requiring specialized vocabulary toward the back of the book.

The topics in the units have been included because they lend themselves to discussion. This means of course that some of these topics are controversial. If the topics were not controversial or would not naturally elicit a variety of opinions, they would not be good discussion starters. One way to lessen the chance of "forcing" a controversial topic on a group of students is to have the students themselves choose which units they would like to cover in the course. It is recommended that the teacher choose one unit to begin the term and that one of the students' first assignments be to form small groups of three to five students to discuss and then rank the topics (i.e., units) in the textbook in terms of which units they would like to do first. This has numerous benefits for the class. First, the teacher is no longer dictating the course. Second, the students have a stronger sense of community. Third, this task itself requires speaking and negotiating practice using spoken English. Finally, students are likely to have better discussions if they are interested in the topics that are being discussed.

Communication Activities

At the back of this text, there are 59 communication activities. These are an essential part of almost every unit. In a given exercise in a unit, students are often told to work in pairs or small groups. Student A will be told to look at one communication activity, while student B will be told to look at another communication activity. In this way, the students hold different pieces of information that only they know and that they must share verbally with their partners. Since the two pieces of information are not on the same page or even near each other in the text, the students must talk to their partners to complete the given language task.

It is essential that students understand the whole activity before teachers have students do the communication activities. The teacher should give an overview of the exercise, explain how the communication task will work, divide the class into pairs or groups as the exercise instructions indicate, and then walk around the room to help any student who might still have questions.

Fluency versus Accuracy in Language Learning

All exercises that are done in any language class are done for accuracy, for fluency, or for a combination of the two. However, we teachers very often tend to do one to the exclusion of the other, and much of what we do, especially what we have traditionally done at the lower levels, is heavily oriented toward accuracy. In contrast, the lessons in *First Discussion Starters* offer a balance of accuracy exercises with fluency exercises.

For an exercise to be fluency oriented, the exercise should be slightly below the actual level of the students so that the students can practice extensively without becoming too distracted by difficult or unfamiliar vocabulary and grammatical points. In other words, the students should find the language level in the exercise easy. The purpose of a fluency exercise is to increase the volume of actual language practice that students can accomplish in the given time limitations. Having the students write out their opinions ahead of time, as many of the exercises require, will allow the students to concentrate their efforts on actual speaking rather than on reading, listening, or vocabulary. Students will learn to speak about a topic in English by doing just that—actually spending class time speaking.

Integrated Skills

Having students write something on the topic before they discuss the topic is innovative and integrates writing and speaking. Although this book is designed primarily to encourage speaking, it calls for other skills such as reading, writing, listening, working in groups, and cooperative learning, yet this is accomplished without students having to do an extensive amount of outside reading or writing, which allows the students to focus on the primary goal of this text: speaking fluency and discussion skills.

Vocabulary Development

Regardless of any ESL or EFL student's level, vocabulary development is one of the primary concerns of many students. To help students acquire and retain important new vocabulary that pertains to the topics presented in the units of *First Discussion Starters,* each unit concludes with a vocabulary check called Language Review. Though this vocabulary information is presented as a review exercise, it may be helpful (or necessary for some lower-proficiency groups) for students to see this vocabulary before beginning the discussion. Whether vocabulary is done as a review, a preview, or both is left up to the individual teacher since no one knows the students and what they can handle better than the actual classroom teacher.

The format for this vocabulary exercise varies from unit to unit. Examples of the different formats follow.

Key word

Read the key word (in bold) in the left column. Circle the letter of the choice that is related to the key word.

1. **split**   a. help   b. divide   c. decorate
2. **annual**   a. once a day b. once a month   c. once a year

Sentence Completion

Circle the best word to complete the sentences.

1. The governor (pressed, passed, asked) a law that prohibits smoking in public places.
2. I saw a very (gentle, stupid, vicious) dog, so I walked away from it.

Definition

Match the words in the left column with their definitions in the right column.

Vocabulary   *Definition*

___ 1. specialist   a. person who focuses on one particular area of study

___ 2. complained   b. to put steady force on something

___ 3. press   c. spoke unhappily

Answer Key

The answers for Language Review, the last exercise in each of the 24 units, and for crossword puzzles are provided at the back of the book. These answers are provided so that the students may check their own work. Logically, it is supposed that the students will use the key only after they have actually completed the exercise. It is further hoped that students will return to the exercise to detect the source of their error to complete the learning process.

Advice from the Authors to the Students

We hope that you will enjoy the topics and activities in this book! Here are some tips and suggestions for using this book to improve your speaking skills in English.

Some people are naturally good at speaking about certain topics. The natural tendency of these extroverted people is to start a topic for discussion. These people have good skills in maintaining the discussion, too. Other people are more quiet and reserved. They may have many ideas to add to the topic, but their natural tendency is to listen. These introverted people are participating in the discussion, too, but in a different way. Regardless of your personality type, you CAN be an active participant in discussions in English. You CAN become a better speaker in English.

In order to improve your discussion skills in English, here are some tips that we strongly recommend.

1. Learn everything you can about the topic because people who are good discussion participants have solid background knowledge of the topic;
2. Learn the vocabulary associated with that topic because you cannot discuss a topic well if you do not know the basic vocabulary for that topic;
3. Learn to use key phrases that allow you to begin discussions (see examples below);
4. Learn to use key phrases that allow you to maintain discussions (see examples below);
5. Learn to use key phrases that make others talk because a discussion NEVER involves just you—without other people you have NO discussion (see examples below);
6. Learn to be a good listener by showing respect for others in your group, which means that you should let everyone speak and you should not interrupt others;
7. Learn to be tolerant of others' ideas because it is this VARIETY of ideas that makes a discussion interesting;
8. Do all of the written prediscussion assignments in this book because research in foreign language studies shows that preparation activities that

require you to write out your ideas will greatly improve the quality and quantity of the language that you produce in class discussions the next day.

Useful Expressions for Starting, Maintaining, and Ending a Discussion

To begin a discussion
- What do you think about _____?
- Do you think _____ is a good thing?
- This topic makes me mad. (explain why)
- I can't believe there are people who think . . . (Explain your position.)

To state your opinion
- I think _____ is a good thing.
- I don't think _____ is a good thing.

To maintain a discussion
- Are there any other ideas on _____?
- Who else agrees with (name)?
- Does anyone else have anything to add to what (name) just said?
- Can anyone else think of another reason to support this idea?
- You know, that's an interesting point that you've just made. (Offer your own opinion now.)

To bring someone else's ideas into the discussion
- (name), what do you think about _____?
- Does anyone else have anything to add?

To assess agreement
- OK, so how many people are in favor of _____?
- How many people agree with what (name) just said?
- OK, is this what the rest of you think, too?

To indicate agreement
- I agree with (name).
- I agree with what (name) just said.
- I think that's right. (Explain your own position now.)

To indicate disagreement in a polite way
- I understand what you (or name) are (is) saying, but I think . . .
- I understand what you (or name) are (is) saying, but I wonder if you have considered (another reason or another idea).
- Hmmm . . . That's interesting, but I wonder if you have considered . . .

To contrast two views on an issue
- Most of us agree that the best decision is to _____. What are some of the reasons that other people might have for disagreeing with this?
- OK, we've heard one side of the issue. What is the other side?

To summarize a discussion
- OK, we're almost out of time. Where do we stand on this topic?
- OK, some of the people think that _____ and others think that _____. (Fill in the blanks with different ideas.)
- _____ and _____ (names of people) think that _____, but _____ and _____ (names of people) think that _____.
- OK, so what is the consensus of our group?
- Do we have a consensus?
- It looks like we'll have to agree to disagree on this topic because our opinions are too far apart.

Useful Grammar Structures for Starting, Maintaining, and Ending a Discussion

1. How to ask a *yes-no* question
   a. verb *to be; can, could, should, will:* move the subject to the second position
      - Are you sure about that?
      - Is that your real opinion?
      - Was he guilty?
      - Were the tickets real?
      - Can you repeat that?
      - Should he go to jail for the rest of his life?
   b. other verbs: use *do, does,* or *did* in the first position
      - Do you think that the woman stole the money?
      - Does a criminal have any rights in jail?
      - Did the police do the correct thing?

2. How to make a negative statement

a. verb *to be; can, could, should, will:* put *not* after (or use a contraction)
- I am not sure about this. (I'm not)
- That is not a serious problem in that country. (isn't)
- He was not guilty. (wasn't)
- The tickets were not real. (weren't)
- People can not go to jail for that kind of crime. (can't)
- The police should not treat people like that. (shouldn't)

b. other verbs: use *do, does,* or *did* with *not* (or use a contraction)
- A criminal does not have any rights in jail. (doesn't)
- My family did not travel a lot when I was young. (didn't)
- Doctors do not have the right to make that decision. (don't)

3. How to ask information (*wh-*) questions
- Who called the police?
- Where did the boy grow up?
- Why do some people disagree with the judge's decision?
- Which unit is the most interesting to you?
- What does this word mean?
- When do most people take their vacation?
- How much did that item cost?
- How many people are there in your family?
- How far is the bank from here?

4. How to express past tense

a. regular verbs: add *-ed*
- played, realized, spelled, believed, snowed, rained (pronounced \d\)
- cooked, walked, laughed, worked, missed, watched (pronounced \t\)
- needed, wanted, created, decided, reacted, added (pronounced \ɪd\ or /əd/)

b. irregular verbs: various endings (must be memorized)
- drove, wrote, woke, ran (one vowel change)
- put, cut, cost (no change)
- ate, taught, bought, caught, did, saw, told, said, went (total change)
- read (pronunciation change but no spelling change)

5. How to combine two "equal" ideas

a. *and:* when you want to add another idea
- The police chased the man, and then they caught him.

b. *but:* when you want to add an idea that is different from the first idea
- The police chased the man, but they couldn't catch him.

c. *so:* when you want to say that one idea is the result of the first one
  • The police caught the thief, so they put him in jail.
d. *so:* when you want to express a purpose
  • The police chased the man so they could arrest him.
e. *or:* when you want to express two options
  • The man should go to jail, or the government should kill him.

6. How to include one idea inside another idea
  a. noun clauses
    • I believe that she is innocent.
    • I don't know why she did that.
    • Can you tell me if that was a good plan?
    • He said that you agree with the judge's decision.
  b. adjective clauses
    • The man that robbed the bank went to jail.
    • I prefer the plan that you talked about.
    • A person who can tell a joke well is a treasure.
  c. adverb clauses
    • When the winner was announced, she shouted for joy!
    • After the jury reached a decision, the murderer cried.
    • Before he goes to the dentist, he always gets pretty nervous.

7. How to express condition
  a. present or everyday routine actions
    • When it rains too much, we don't play tennis.
    • When I was late, my boss got mad.
  b. present unreal condition
    • If I had a million dollars, I would buy a new car for you.
    • If we spoke more languages, that would be a very good thing.
  c. past unreal conditions
    • If I had studied, I would have passed the exam today.
    • If a student had complained about the magazines, the school would have removed them.

A Serious Problem with a Pet

An Akita

Exercise 1.1

Read this true story about a dog.

> In 1991, an Akita dog named Taro bit a young girl on her lip. The girl was a niece of Taro's owner, so the dog knew or had seen the girl before. In 1987, the state of New Jersey passed a new law that said that the owners of pit bulls, another breed of dog, had to restrain or control their dogs.

The wound that Taro caused was not so serious. However, Taro was guilty of biting the girl (which was true) and was sentenced to death under this 1987 law.

Brigitte Bardot, the famous French actress who became an international animal rights activist, pleaded for the New Jersey state governor to be lenient and not kill Taro. Taro's owner spent thousands of dollars on lawyers for the dog. Even the Japanese government asked for leniency and offered to let Taro live in Japan. (Akitas are a breed that originated in Japan.)

The man who first suggested this dog law, Joseph Azzolina, said that Taro should live. He said that the court's decision was "as ridiculous as it is unbelievable, since my law was meant to affect only vicious pit bulls and other dogs that attack humans."

Exercise 1.2

What do you think? Do you think Taro should be killed? Why or why not? (Give at least two reasons.)

_____

_____

_____

_____

_____

_____

_____

_____

_____

Exercise 1.3

Work in pairs or small groups. Discuss your answers to exercise 1.2. When you finish, read communication activity 13 to find out what the court decided.

Exercise 1.4

Read the following statements and indicate your reactions by circling 1 if you *agree strongly*, 2 if you *agree somewhat*, 3 if you are *not sure*, 4 if you *disagree somewhat*, and 5 if you *disagree strongly*. Then write your opinions about these statements. Be sure to include one or two reasons to explain your opinions.

a. 1   2   3   4   5   Some people treat their pets better than they treat other people.

_____

_____

_____

_____

_____

_____

b. 1 2 3 4 5   It's all right for people to bring their pets into public places such as supermarkets and restaurants.

_____

_____

_____

_____

_____

c. 1 2 3 4 5   A cat or dog is a good pet, but a snake is not a good pet.

_____

_____

_____

_____

d. 1 2 3 4 5   It's OK to use your own spoon at dinner to take food from your plate, put it to your pet's mouth, let it eat, and then continue to use the spoon yourself.

_____

_____

_____

_____

e. 1 2 3 4 5   People can communicate with their pets, and the pets can communicate with their owners.

_____

_____

_____

_____

_____

f. 1 2 3 4 5   It is all right for people to bring their pets with them when they travel on airplanes.

_____

_____

_____

_____

_____

Exercise 1.5

Now work in small groups to compare and discuss your answers to exercise 1.4.

Exercise 1.6

Write about any pet that you had or that you still have. What kind of animal is/was it? What is/was its name? How old is/was your pet? How did you get your pet? Why do/did you have a pet?

_____

_____

_____

_____

_____

_____

_____

_____

Exercise 1.7

Now work in pairs or small groups. Take turns describing your pets. When each person finishes speaking, the listener has an obligation to ask questions about the parts that the listener did not understand. Which person gave the most surprising answer?

Exercise 1.8

Fluency Practice

In this activity, you will do the same thing that you did in exercise 1.7, but you will do this with a different partner or small group. This gives you a chance to practice saying the same information more than once and to give a presentation more than one time.

Language Review

Circle the best word to complete the sentences.

1. The governor (pressed, passed, asked) a law that prohibits smoking in public places.

2. A poodle is a (breed, size, brand) of dog that originated in France. This type of dog has curly hair.

3. The animal was very angry, and its owners couldn't (repeat, restrain, feed) it. The dog was able to get away from its owner.

4. The young boy had a terrible (wound, anger, smile) on his face, so he had to go to the doctor for help.

5. She said she was innocent, but everyone believed that she was (guilty, unhappy, true).

6. The judge (described, explained, sentenced) the robber to 10 years in prison.

7. Brigitte Bardot is an animal rights (artist, actress, activist) who wants to protect animals from bad treatment by humans.

8. The prisoner asked the judge to be (punished, guilty, lenient). He wanted the judge to have mercy on him and be gentle.

9. I saw a very (gentle, stupid, vicious) dog, so I walked away from it.

10. It is important for people to (give, take, treat) each other with respect and behave politely.

11. I think that it's rude for people to talk on their cell phones in (private, public, quiet) places such as a supermarket, a restaurant, or a bank.

12. The young girl (described, thought about, asked) the situation to her mother.

13. The dog (owned, became, bit) the girl, and that is what started the whole problem.

14. He (suggested, let, spent) me use his car.

15. The idea that people can live to be two hundred years old is (ridiculous, serious, sentenced).

16. She is my (human, government, niece).

17. Do you believe her story? Do you think that her story is (lenient, true, state)?

18. I (became, spent, let) a teacher for many reasons.

19. Oh, no! He cut his (breed, lip, law).

20. Who is the (activist, governor, owner) of that dog?

UNIT 2

Should We Censor These Popular Magazines?

A typical waiting room in an office

Exercise 2.1

Read this true story about an intensive English school in the United States. It was written by James T. Raby at Clark University in Worcester, Massachusetts.

At our Intensive English Program, we subscribe to a wide variety of magazines. We make these magazines available to our students, much as magazines are available in the waiting rooms of doctors' offices. These magazines are not used in classes, and students are free to read them or ignore them. They are for extra English practice. Some of these magazines are about science. Others are about business, and others are general interest. The fact is that we have a wide variety of types of magazines for our students. The main focus of one of these magazines is on pop culture. It deals with celebrities and topics that appeal to college-age students. (Most of our students are college-age students. None is younger, but a few are older.) Lately this magazine has been coming with seminude models on the cover. Certain parts of the body are always strategically covered, but there is no doubt that the models are unclothed. My question is: *Should we remove this magazine from circulation in our program?*

There are two sides to this question. Some say that we should censor the magazines. Some staff say that some of our students from the Middle East, for example, might find the magazines offensive. I've spent time in the Middle East myself and remember buying news magazines that had covers that had been torn off and text and photos blackened over by the censors. I don't want to contribute to that sort of atmosphere here, but neither do I want to offend people. Other staff members say that the students are in the United States now and these magazines are normal for this country. They point out that we are not forcing any students to read these magazines. It's optional extra help, and there are many kinds of magazines besides this one.

We are not sure what to do. Should we censor the magazines? Or should we do nothing? What advice do you have for us?

Exercise 2.2

What is your opinion about this problem? What should the director do? Write your opinion about this and explain your reasons. Be sure to give at least two or three reasons.

_____

_____

_____

_____

_____

_____

_____

_____

_____

_____

_____

_____

_____

Exercise 2.3

Consider the other point of view on this issue. Write two reasons to support
the opinion that is the opposite of the opinion that you gave in exercise 2.2.
For example, if you think the school should control the magazines better, what
are two reasons why they should *not* control the magazines?

1. _____

   _____

2. _____

   _____

Exercise 2.4

Now work in pairs or small groups and take turns discussing your opinions
about this important matter. Discuss your answers from exercises 2.2 and 2.3.
Should the school control the magazines more carefully? Or should the students themselves have to choose what they read or don't read?

Exercise 2.5

It might be interesting to hear what teachers at other schools say about this situation. Read communication activities 3 and 29 and then write two or three
sentences to summarize what the teacher says. What does the teacher suggest?
(*Note:* This is a good homework activity.)

Communication Activity 3

Name of teacher: ———————————————————

School: ———————————————————

Location: ———————————————————

Opinion: ————————————————————

————————————————————

————————————————————

————————————————————

————————————————————

Communication Activity 29

Name of teacher: ———————————————————

School: ———————————————————

Location: ———————————————————

Opinion: ————————————————————

————————————————————

————————————————————

————————————————————

Exercise 2.6

Work in groups or as a class. Discuss your reaction to the two teachers' comments. Has your opinion of this changed?

Exercise 2.7

When you have finished all of the discussion on this topic, look at communication activity 49 to see what the school actually did about this matter.

Exercise 2.8

Read the following statements and indicate your reactions by circling 1 if you *agree strongly,* 2 if you *agree somewhat,* 3 if you are *not sure,* 4 if you *disagree somewhat,* and 5 if you *disagree strongly.* Then write your opinions about these statements. Be sure to include one or two reasons to explain your opinions.

a. 1   2   3   4   5   The government should ban some kinds of books that have pictures of naked people.

_____

_____

b. 1   2   3   4   5   Young people's books that explain facts about sex should not be allowed in elementary school libraries.

_____

_____

c. 1   2   3   4   5   The government should have a list of "sensitive" topics that should not be discussed in the newspaper or on television.

_____

_____

d. 1   2   3   4   5   It is acceptable to ban songs that contain language that is too strong.

_____

_____

e. 1   2   3   4   5   TV ads for alcohol and cigarettes should be banned.

_____

_____

f. 1 2 3 4 5 Nobody has the right to decide what I can read or listen to. This is my decision alone.

_____

_____

Exercise 2.9

Work in small groups to discuss your answers to exercise 2.8. Which questions have the widest range of answers? Can your group reach an agreement on any of these questions?

Exercise 2.10

Role Play

Work in small groups.

Scene: A student complained to the school director about the covers and the pictures of some of the magazines that are routinely on the tables in the office. To try to resolve the problem, the people involved gather for an honest discussion of the situation. Possible participants: the student who complained; a student who likes the magazines; a teacher whose main concern is English, English, and English; the school director; the student's parent; a teacher at the school.

Your role:

_____

Your position on this issue:

_____

_____

_____

_____

_____

_____

_____

_____

_____

_____

_____

Language Review

Read the key word or phrase (in bold) in the left column. Circle the letter of the choice that is related to the key word or phrase.

1. **occasional**   a. often   b. sometimes   c. never

2. **audience**   a. prohibit   b. show   c. choose

3. **adapt**   a. change   b. understand   c. like

4. **plenty**   a. enough   b. too little   c. too much

5. **conservative**   a. unusual   b. traditional   c. negative

6. **handle**   a. like   b. dislike   c. accept

7. **get accustomed   a. become   b. become   c. become
   to**   familiar   famous   unhappy

8. **overlapped**   a. destroyed   b. helped   c. covered

9. **censor**   a. protect   b. ban   c. provide

10. **subscribe to**   a. buy regularly   b. buy sometimes c. never buy

11. **variety**   a. similarity   b. difference   c. uniqueness

12. **ignore**   a. visit   b. avoid   c. read

13. **celebrities**   a. rich people   b. famous people c. sick people

14. **topics**   a. subjects   b. stars   c. covers

15. **appeal to**   a. be hated by   b. be liked by   c. be asked by

16. **semi-** (prefix)   a. mostly   b. partly   c. completely

17. **lately**   a. yearly   b. recently   c. only

18. **strategically**   a. carelessly   b. carefully   c. unusually

19. **contribute**   a. be a part of   b. be different from   c. go against

20. **sort of**   a. top of   b. type of   c. bottom of

21. **atmosphere**   a. environment   b. sky   c. world

22. **force**   a. require   b. request   c. allow

23. **optional**   a. demanded   b. required   c. chosen

24. **remove**   a. move again   b. take away   c. drive fast

25. **the cover**   a. the bottom   b. the middle   c. the top

Put the Story Together: Mommy's White Hair

Exercise 3.1

Can you guess what happened? Work in groups of seven.* Each student will have a piece of the story. Try to put the story together.

Step 1. Each student should look at one of these communication activities: 4, 12, 20, 28, 35, 44, 52.

---

*If there are extra students, these students should be judges. The judges should listen to the story lines and decide if the seven students have put themselves in the correct order or not. Conversely, if there are not seven students, the teacher should participate, and perhaps one or two of the lines could be copied on a sheet of paper that could be placed on the floor in the correct position within the story. (See step 4.)

Step 2. Write your activity number in the box and write your sentence on the lines.

☐ _____

_____

Step 3. You have one minute to read and memorize your piece of the story. You do not have to use the exact same words, but you need to express the same idea.

Step 4. The seven students should stand up and put themselves (i.e., their pieces of the story) in order by taking turns saying (not reading) their lines aloud.

Exercise 3.2

For homework, write another strip story like the one in exercise 3.1. Do not have more than ten lines; fewer lines are OK if you have a smaller class. Try to have a funny ending. Write one copy of your story on a sheet of paper and make another copy that you will cut up into strips to give to students.

Exercise 3.3

When you were a child, did you behave well? _____ What are some of the things that you did that bothered your mother and father?

_____

_____

_____

_____

_____

_____

_____

Exercise 3.4

Work in small groups. Discuss your answers to the questions in exercise 3.3.

Language Review

Match the words in the left column with their definitions in the right column.

	Vocabulary	*Definition*
___	1. a few	a. change from one thing to another
___	2. turn	b. disturb or annoy
___	3. a minute	c. a small number
___	4. behave	d. a short time
___	5. bother	e. act a certain way
___	6. quiet	f. a room where people cook
___	7. thought	g. looked at
___	8. kitchen	h. a plate
___	9. wrong	i. no sound or music
___	10. angry	j. not happy; upset; mad
___	11. saw	k. not right
___	12. a dish	l. believed

Be sure to visit <www.press.umich.edu/esl> for ideas on related Web sites, videos, and other activities.

UNIT 4

Group Speaking Puzzle: Professions

What is the best profession? Why?

Exercise 4.1

Work in groups of three. Student A should look at communication activity 5; student B, 27; and student C, 54. Each of these communication activities contains clues to some of the answers to the crossword puzzle.

Step 1. Use the clues in your communication activity to solve the puzzle.
Step 2. When you have used all your clues, you and your two partners should ask each other for clues about the answers that you do not know. Do not look at your partners' communication activities during this step. It is okay to use the clues from the communication activities, but you may not refer to the communication activities themselves. Try to make up your own descriptions for the answers whenever possible. Do not tell the answers directly to anyone and do not spell any of the letters of the answers.

Exercise 4.2

After you finish the puzzle, work in small groups. Discuss your answers to these questions.

1. Number 1 across is a doctor for your teeth. Many people hate to go to the dentist's office. Are you one of these people? Why or why not?
2. What is the difference between number 8 across and number 14 across? Is anyone in your family in one of these professions? Why did that person choose this profession?
3. Think about number 18 across. This profession has a high salary. Do you think that you could do this job? Why or why not?

4. Think about number 19 across. People in this profession earn a very high salary. Do you think that you could do this job? Why or why not?

5. Number 19 down is a kind of class. When you were in school, did you have this kind of class? Did you like it? Why or why not?

6. Number 21 across is an interesting profession. Have you ever taken your pet to the vet's office? What happened? Describe the vet that you saw there.

7. Number 2 down is a very important profession. Do you think you could be a teacher? Why or why not? How are teachers in your culture different from those in the United States?

8. If you could choose the top three professions that you would like as your career, what would they be? Compare answers with your classmates.

9. Can you think of a profession that was important one hundred years ago but that is no longer important or common now? Why is this profession no longer common?

10. What profession do you think will be important in society in 20 years? Fifty years? One hundred years?

 Language Review

Read the key word or phrase (in bold) in the left column. Circle the letter of the choice that is related to the key word or phrase.

1. **engineer**   a. motor   b. hospital   c. building

2. **pilot**   a. fly   b. farmer   c. relax

3. **vet**   a. animals   b. trucks   c. passengers

4. **dentist**   a. student   b. course   c. teeth

5. **butcher**   a. butter   b. meat   c. dessert

6. **grow up**   a. teacher → student   b. child → adult   c. hot → cold

7. **nurse**   a. medicines   b. letters   c. watches

8. **farm**   a. clouds   b. animals   c. museum

9. **salary**   a. money   b. telephone   c. automobile

10. **pig**   a. hospital   b. river   c. animal

11. **uniform**   a. papers   b. clothes   c. ideas

12. **opposite**   a. different   b. active   c. helpful

13. **build**   a. a house   b. a book   c. a dinner

14. **quick**   a. not nice   b. not cheap   c. not slow

15. **abbreviation** a. $ b. etc.   c. you and I

16. **fast**   a. not nice   b. not cheap   c. not slow

17. **floor**   a. farm   b. building   c. profession

18. **get well**   a. old → not old   b. sick → not sick   c. big → not big

19. **cousin**   a. person   b. thing   c. idea

20. **earn**   a. training   b. money   c. food

Ten Proverbs

When in Rome, do as the Romans do.

What is a proverb? A proverb is a special expression. This special expression has an important message. Sometimes this message is easy to see; other times you have to think very hard about the meanings of the words before you can understand the real message.

Many times the literal or exact meanings of the words in the proverbs do not explain the meanings of the proverbs themselves. For example, what does the proverb "When in Rome, do as the Romans do" mean? Are we talking about people from Rome? Are we talking only about Romans?

The real meaning of this proverb is that when you are in a different place, you should do what people there do. If you go to a country where everyone arrives late, then you should arrive late. If you go to someone's house where they do not eat meat, you should eat the food that they give you and not make any comments about not having meat. The general meaning is that you should see what the people around you are doing and follow their actions or customs.

Proverbs are interesting because they teach us things about a country or culture. For example, in many English-speaking countries, there are many proverbs about time and money. One could argue, therefore, that time and money are very important parts of these cultures.

Exercise 5.1

There are five groups of proverbs below (group 1, group 2, group 3, group 4, group 5). Each student will read the two proverbs in ONE of the five groups and then try to guess the meanings of those two proverbs. Write your guesses on the lines.

Group 1
a. Beauty is only skin deep.

_____

_____

b. It is better to give than to receive.

_____

_____

Group 2
a. Do unto others as you would like them to do unto you.

_____

_____

b. If you want to keep a friend, never borrow, never lend.

_____

_____

Group 3
a. First impressions are the most lasting.

_____

_____

b. It's better to be safe than sorry.

_____

_____

Group 4
a. There is no time like the present.

_____

_____

b. If you lie down with dogs, you will get up with fleas.

_____

_____

Group 5
a. Don't wash your dirty linen in public.

_____

_____

b. There are plenty of other fish in the sea.

_____

_____

Exercise 5.2

After you finish exercise 5.1, work in groups of three or four students who all wrote about the same group of proverbs. Students should take turns saying what they wrote for the meaning of each proverb.

When you have finished discussing your possible meanings, check your answers in the following communication activities. Group 1 should read communication activity 7, group 2 should read communication activity 23, group 3 should read communication activity 34, group 4 should read communication activity 47, and group 5 should read communication activity 55.

Exercise 5.3

Write all ten proverbs on the board. Take turns explaining the proverbs one at a time. It is important for the students to present the meanings of these proverbs. The teacher can help if more information is needed.

Exercise 5.4

Think about the proverbs in the previous exercises. Write two situations, one that explains the first proverb that you wrote about in exercise 5.1 and one that explains the second proverb you wrote about. At the end of each situation, write the proverb on the line provided.

Situation 1

_____

_____

Proverb

_____

Situation 2

_____

_____

_____

_____

_____

_____

_____

_____

_____

_____

_____

_____

Proverb

_____

Exercise 5.5

Work in small groups (three to five students is best). Make sure you have students who were not in your original group in exercise 5.2. Take turns reading your situation aloud (or just telling your situation if you can remember the details). After a person has told the situation, the others should try to guess what the proverb is.

Exercise 5.6

Write down a proverb in your native or another language. Translate the words (literal translation) and see if anyone from a different language background can guess the meaning of the proverb. Then work with a native speaker to see if you can find an English proverb that has a similar meaning. (Sometimes the English translation will be very similar to the native language original, but sometimes it will be very different.)

In another language:

_____

Literal translation:

_____

Equivalent English proverb:

_____

 Language Review

Read the key word or phrase (in bold) in the left column. Circle the letter of the choice that is related to the key word or phrase.

1. **proverb**   a. special day   b. special expression   c. special idea

2. **literal**   a. exact meaning   b. similar meaning   c. no meaning

3. **unto**   a. for   b. with   c. to

4. **borrow**   a. 100 minutes   b. 100 dollars   c. 100 people

5. **lend**   a. give money   b. ask for money   c. take money

6. **impression**   a. effect or feeling   b. word or phrase   c. day or time

7. **lasting**   a. calling   b. continuing   c. confusing

8. **flea**　　　　　a. small animal　　b. small insect　　c. small dog

9. **linen**　　　　a. hats　　　　　　b. shoes　　　　　c. bedsheets

10. **public**　　　a. not private　　　b. not interesting　c. not quiet

11. **plenty**　　　a. too much　　　　b. not always　　　c. enough

12. **surface**　　a. on the outside　b. on the inside　c. in the middle

13. **physical**　　a. about the body　b. about the mind　c. about God

14. **characteristic**　a. anyone; someone　b. quality; trait　c. proverb; saying

15. **gossip**　　　a. talk about life　b. talk about a person　c. talk quickly

16. **put off**　　a. postpone　　　　b. prepare　　　　c. decide

17. **the present**　a. now　　　　　　b. tomorrow　　　c. yesterday

18. **better**　　　a. delicious　　　　b. expensive　　　c. good

19. **safe**　　　　a. not dangerous　b. not interesting　c. not healthy

20. **skin**　　　　a. water　　　　　b. body　　　　　c. sofa

21. **sea**　　　　　a. look　　　　　　b. ocean　　　　　c. plant

22. **previous**　　a. after　　　　　　b. now　　　　　c. before

Jail for Parents of Absent Students?

Who is responsible?

Exercise 6.1

Read this passage about students who do not follow rules.

"Cutting school"* is a common practice for many students. Rather than going to school, students go to the mall, the beach, or a nearby friend's house. Some students cut class a lot, and teachers and administrators are worried. In particular, teachers are worried because when students get low grades, teachers are often blamed. However, teachers are saying that the responsibility of coming to class belongs to the student. Teachers are saying that they are not responsible for the poor grades that these students are getting.

---

*Other common expressions for this are "playing hookey" and "skipping school."

There are disagreements as to where the responsibility for poor attendance lies. Some parents believe that it is the responsibility of the school to make sure that students attend school every day. At the same time, some teachers feel it is the parents' responsibility to make sure that the children attend school. However, parents say that they do not have the power to force their high-school-age children to go to school. Parents say that their children leave the house for school but just go somewhere else instead.

The state of Illinois has enacted a law that offers a controversial solution to this problem.

Exercise 6.2

Think of three possible answers for this question: What solution did the state of Illinois offer? Write your three answers on the lines below. Circle the number of your best answer. Be prepared to explain why you think your answer is a good solution to the problem of class absences.

1. _____

_____

2. _____

_____

3. _____

_____

Exercise 6.3

Work in small groups. Take turns presenting your three ideas. Tell which one you think is your best answer. Then each group should choose its best answer (or two) from exercise 6.2 and tell it to the class. Be ready to give reasons to support your answer. Which answer do most people think is the best one? Discuss the advantages and disadvantages of each suggestion. When you finish, read the state's real decision in communication activity 25.

Exercise 6.4

What do you think about the State of Illinois's decision? Write your opinion and one or two reasons for your opinion here.

_____

_____

_____

_____

_____

_____

_____

_____

_____

Exercise 6.5

Work in small groups. Discuss your opinion and your reasons from exercise 6.4. What is the general opinion of the members of your group?

Exercise 6.6

Some people say that parents of misbehaving teenagers should be held responsible for their children's actions. These people believe that making parents responsible will make parents take a more active role in their children's lives. This will build better values and teach the children to know right from wrong. Write three (or more) reasons why it is correct to hold parents responsible for their children's actions.

_____

_____

_____

_____

_____

_____

_____

_____

_____

_____

_____

However, many people disagree with the idea of holding parents responsible for actions that happen outside their homes. Consider this opposing view. Write two or three reasons that people might have for disagreeing with what you have written above.

_____

_____

_____

_____

_____

_____

_____

_____

_____

Exercise 6.7

In small groups, discuss your answers and opinions given in exercise 6.6. Is your group able to agree? In the end, are parents responsible for their children's actions?

Exercise 6.8

Read this story about a student and her parent in Florida.

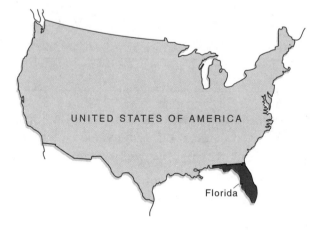

In 1999, Kimberly Barbey of St. Petersburg, Florida, was put in jail because her third-grade daughter, age nine, missed 161 days (of 180) in the 1998–99 school year and missed 9 days of the first 19 school days of the 1999–2000 school year.

A county judge, Patrick Cadell, decided to put Barbey in jail because Barbey's daughter had too many absences. The judge believed that the number of absences was an abuse of the system. It was a violation of Florida law.

The school principal, Terry Krasner, said, "The intent was never to see a mother in jail." The school tried to help Barbey and her child. The school sent a guidance counselor, a social worker, and a nurse to the home several times.

Ron Stone, a spokesperson for the school district, said, "Most parents, once you talk about legal action, they get the child in school." Barbey received warnings about this matter in court several times.

Some people in the area were shocked that a parent was sent to jail for something that the child did, but two years earlier, there was a similar case. Near Tampa, Florida, a mother was put in jail for two months for letting her daughter miss 315 days of school between 1995 and 1998.

Exercise 6.9

What do you think of this Florida case? Do you agree or disagree with the judges'
decisions to put the mothers in jail? Why?

_____

_____

_____

_____

_____

_____

_____

_____

Exercise 6.10

Work in small groups. Discuss your opinion of the Florida judge's decision in
the Barbey case. Is this case similar to or different from the problem that the
Illinois law was designed to solve?

Exercise 6.11

Your Childhood

Answer these questions about how your parents treated you in terms of responsibility.

1. Were your parents strict with you? _____

_____

2. If you made a mistake or misbehaved, what did your parents do? Give specific examples.

_____

_____

_____

3. Did they give you specific responsibilities when you were a child? If so, give examples.

_____

_____

4. Compared to your brothers or sisters, did your parents give you more or less responsibility?

_____

_____

5. Why do you think this is true?

_____

_____

_____

6. When you compare it to the situations of other people in your culture, do you think your situation with your parents and responsibility was usual? If not, what was different?

_____

_____

_____

Exercise 6.12

Work in pairs or small groups. Discuss your answers about responsibility when you were a child.

Language Review

Read the key word or phrase (in bold) in the left column. Circle the letter of the choice that is related to the key word or phrase.

1. **occasional**   a. often   b. always   c. sometimes

2. **strict**   a. rules   b. classes   c. lines

3. **attend**   a. stay away from   b. go to   c. look at

4. **misbehave**   a. behave badly   b. behave politely   c. want to see

5. **practice**   a. repeated effort   b. natural ability   c. knowledge

6. **rather than**   a. in addition to   b. because of   c. instead of

7. **administration**   a. employees   b. management   c. teachers

8. **cut class**   a. not do well   b. not understand   c. not attend

9. **blame**   a. "You did it!"   b. "I love you!"   c. "He is great!"

10. **make sure**   a. be angry   b. be certain   c. be patient

11. **too many**   a. a few   b. some   c. too big a number

12. **shocked**   a. believed   b. warned   c. surprised

13. **this matter**   a. situation   b. people   c. transportation

14. **daughter**   a. son   b. sun   c. some

15. **earlier**   a. after   b. now   c. before

You Can Be the Judge:
The $1,100,000 Lottery Jackpot

Exercise 7.1

Read this court case about a divorce.

Herman and Viola Alston separated in 1985. Two years later, in 1987, Viola Alston filed for divorce. In her divorce petition (request), Mrs. Alston did not seek alimony or a share of the couple's property. At that time, Mrs. Alston was a clerk with the federal government and Mr. Alston was a prison guard with the District of Columbia.

A few days after Mrs. Alston filed the papers for a divorce, Mr. Alston had the winning ticket for the Lotto. In fact, the jackpot that he won was over a million dollars: $1.1 million. Under the terms of the lottery prize, he receives $44,000 a year after taxes in lottery payments. Mrs. Alston thought that part of this money should go to her, so she refiled her divorce papers and demanded alimony. (In other words, when Mr. Alston won the lottery, the couple was still married. Mrs. Alston had filed the divorce papers, but Mr. Alston won the lottery before the divorce was final.)

Mrs. Alston said that she did not ask Mr. Alston for anything at the divorce because she knew that he did not have any money or savings.

Exercise 7.2

If you were the judge, what would you do? Does Mr. Alston have to pay half of his prize money (or any part of his prize money) to Mrs. Alston?

_____

_____

_____

Write two or three reasons for your answer.

1. _____

   _____

2. _____

   _____

3. _____

   _____

Exercise 7.3

Work in small groups. Discuss your decision and your reasons. When you finish, read communication activity 22 for the result of the case.

Exercise 7.4

If you won $1,100,000, what would you do with the money? Remember that you have $44,000 each year. You do not get the total amount of money in one payment.

_____

_____

_____

_____

_____

_____

_____

Can you think of any problems that might result because you have won so much money?

_____

_____

_____

_____

Exercise 7.5

Work in groups. Compare your answers to exercise 7.4. Which answers are the most interesting or unusual?

Language Review

Match the vocabulary items in the left column with their definitions in the right column.

Vocabulary   *Definition*

___ 1. divorce   a. a game that people win by chance

___ 2. petition   b. when all the people agree with a decision

___ 3. alimony   c. to end a marriage permanently

___ 4. filed   d. money or property from a divorced spouse

___ 5. ticket   e. protest something; formally disagree

___ 6. jackpot   f. a piece of; a portion of

___ 7. terms   g. a legal document that requests a change

___ 8. lottery   h. relating to the law

___ 9. part   i. legally submitted a document into the system

___ 10. demanded   j. insisted; required

___ 11. appeal   k. a small paper used to enter a game or an event

___ 12. legal   l. rules; requirements

___ 13. unanimous   m. money, usually a large amount, won in a game

___ 14. thought   n. something you win

___ 15. prize   o. past tense of think

___ 16. savings   p. the money that a family puts aside for a special reason

Finish the Story: The Nonsmoking Smoker

Exercise 8.1

Read the following true story about a smoker.

Mila Bertelli, a 47-year-old woman, is a smoker. However, for a period of 58 consecutive hours (almost three days!), she wasn't able to smoke because of the special circumstances that she was in, so she didn't. She spent most of the 58 hours reading the newspaper. When that period of time was up, she started smoking again. During the 58 hours that she did not smoke, she had cigarettes, so that is not the reason that she did not smoke.

Exercise 8.2

Try to think of three possible answers for this question: Why didn't Mila smoke during those 58 hours? Write your three answers on the lines. Circle the number of the explanation that you think is the best one.

1. _____

_____

2. _____

_____

3. _____

_____

Exercise 8.3

Work in small groups. Why didn't Mila smoke during those 58 hours? Discuss your answers for exercise 8.2. All students should give reasons to support their answers. Other students should listen and then say why the reason is possible or not possible in this situation. Then choose the best answer or answers from your group.

Exercise 8.4

Each group should present its best two or three possible answers to the class. Be ready to give reasons to support your answers. When another group presents their answers, ask questions or give facts in order to get more information or show why the answer is not likely.

Exercise 8.5

Hot or Cold?

A panel of "experts" should be chosen from the class. (Perhaps one person from each of the groups can be chosen.) The panel should sit in a row of chairs at the front of the room. Only the panel members should read communication activity 14 to find out the real reason the woman did not smoke. The other students take turns making statements about what they think happened. The panel members can use "hot" or "cold" to say if the students are far from the real answer or close to the real answer. If no progress is being made, the judges (or teacher) may decide to give a few clues to help out the guessers.
Here are some helpful expressions for playing "Hot or Cold."

"You're hot."	=	"You almost have the right answer."
"You're warm."	=	"You're near the answer."
"You're cold."	=	"You are not near the answer at all."
"You're getting warmer."	=	"That is a better answer. You're starting to get the right idea."
"You're getting colder."	=	"You're going away from the answer."

Useful language:
Did the woman . . . ?
Was the woman . . . ?
Was the reason connected to . . . (a noun)?
Did she stop smoking because . . . (subject or verb)?

Language Review

Match the vocabulary items in the left column with their definitions in the right column.

Vocabulary	*Definition*
___ 1. however	a. an apartment that people can buy
___ 2. consecutive	b. but
___ 3. circumstances	c. be unable to move
___ 4. period	d. situation
___ 5. spent	e. a person who knows a lot about one subject
___ 6. expert	f. one after the other
___ 7. clues	g. an area where there are a lot of hotels
___ 8. condominium	h. a piece of time
___ 9. resort	i. past tense of *spend*; used
___ 10. get stuck	j. hints; suggestions for a possible answer
___ 11. (time) is up	k. not usual; not ordinary
___ 12. special	l. finished

Sex Education in Schools: What Are We Teaching Our Children?

Exercise 9.1

Read the following statements about sex education in schools* and indicate your reactions by circling 1 if you *agree strongly*, 2 if you *agree somewhat*, 3 if you are *not sure*, 4 if you *disagree somewhat*, and 5 if you *disagree strongly*. Then write your opinions about these statements. Be sure to include one or two reasons to explain your opinions.

a. 1   2   3   4   5   When children are born, they know everything they need to know about their bodies, including sex.

_____

_____

---

*In this unit, schools means elementary, junior high, and high school.

b. 1 2 3 4 5   Schools should teach children about sex.

_____

_____

c. 1 2 3 4 5   In countries where the schools teach a course called "sex education," girls have more babies than they do in countries without sex education in the schools.

_____

_____

d. 1 2 3 4 5   Sex is a natural behavior, so children don't need to learn about it.

_____

_____

e. 1 2 3 4 5   Parents should teach their children about sex.

_____

_____

f. 1 2 3 4 5   Giving out condoms in high school encourages students to have sex before marriage.

_____

_____

g. 1 2 3 4 5   It is possible to teach students about sex and at the same time encourage them to avoid sex before marriage.

_____

_____

h. 1 2 3 4 5   It does not matter whether sex education comes from parents or from school. The fact is that most information about sex comes from the students' friends.

_____

_____

i. 1 2 3 4 5   High schools should give out condoms to help students protect themselves from diseases.

_____

_____

j. 1 2 3 4 5   It is all right for parents to teach their daughters about sex, but daughters should not receive any sexual information in the schools.

_____

_____

Exercise 9.2

Now work in small groups to discuss your answers to exercise 9.1. Speakers should explain their opinions and the reasons for those opinions. Which questions created the most discussion? __, __, and __

Exercise 9.3

Do you think that students should have to take a course in sex education? _____ Why or why not?

_____

_____

_____

_____

_____

_____

A sex education course can include many different topics, such as information on birth control (including how to take birth control pills and how to put on a condom), anatomy of the human body, prevention of sexually transmitted diseases (including AIDS), and homosexuality. Do you think these topics are suitable (appropriate) for high school students? _____ Why or why not?

_____

_____

_____

_____

_____

Exercise 9.4

Now work in small groups of three to five students. Discuss your answers to exercise 9.3.

 Language Review

Read the key word or phrase (in bold) in the left column. Circle the letter of the choice that is related to the key word or phrase.

1. **be born**   a. come into the world   b. die slowly   c. be disinterested

2. **natural**   a. relating to names   b. relating to nature c. relating to action

3. **behavior**   a. actions   b. thoughts   c. information

4. **suitable**   a. interesting   b. appropriate   c. information

5. **diseases**   a. sicknesses   b. difficulty   c. problems

6. **encourage**   a. defend   b. support   c. require

7. **avoid**   a. stay in front of   b. stay under   c. stay away from

8. **a fact**   a. It is surprising.   b. It is emotional.   c. It is true.

9. **protect**   a. be safe   b. be serious   c. be absent

10. **a course** a. a medicine   b. a class   c. a problem

11. **a condom** a. no sex   b. no baby   c. no education

12. **prevent**   a. stop   b. predict   c. analyze

Freedom of Speech: Who Says?

Exercise 10.1

Read the statements below and decide if you agree or disagree with them. Circle *A* if you agree and *D* if you disagree. Then explain your answers on the lines provided.

1. A   D   People should be free to say anything they want to say, even if it hurts someone else.

_____

_____

2. A   D   People should be free to say anything they want to say only if it doesn't hurt someone else.

_____

_____

3. A   D   If I dislike someone, I should be allowed to say my opinions in public.

_____

_____

4. A   D   People don't have to hear or see things that disturb them.

_____

_____

5. A   D   People outside of my family should be able to tell me how to speak.

_____

_____

6. A   D   My government can tell me what I can and cannot say.

_____

_____

7. A   D   It is acceptable for people to speak disrespectfully about people who are from a different race or ethnic background.

_____

_____

8. A   D   It is acceptable for people to speak disrespectfully about people who have different financial and educational backgrounds.

_____

_____

Exercise 10.2

Work in groups to discuss your answers to exercise 10.1. Do most of the people

in your group agree or disagree with each statement? _____

On which statement do you disagree the most? ___ Why do you disagree on this

statement? _____

_____

_____

_____

_____

_____

Exercise 10.3

Read this situation involving a major league baseball player who received a lot
of attention after he gave his opinion in a national magazine.

During an interview for an article in the
December 1999 issue of *Sports Illustrated*, a
popular sports-themed magazine in the United
States, an Atlanta Braves baseball player created
a great deal of controversy when he gave his
honest opinion to a reporter. The 25-year-old
John Rocker said that he would never play for
a New York baseball team because he didn't

want to ride a subway train "next to some queer with AIDS." He also
said, "I'm not a very big fan of foreigners" and called an African
American teammate a "fat monkey."

Exercise 10.4

After the article was published, major league baseball commissioner Bud Selig
had to decide if John Rocker's words required any punishment by the league.

a. If you were the commissioner, what would you decide? Is John Rocker free to say what he wants, or is he required to keep quiet about his opinions about others?

_____

_____

_____

b. What punishment—if any—do you think John Rocker should receive from the baseball commissioner?

_____

_____

_____

_____

c. Write two or three reasons for your opinion.

_____

_____

_____

_____

_____

_____

_____

_____

_____

Exercise 10.5

Work in small groups. Discuss your opinion and your reasons. When you finish, read the decision in communication activity 56.

Exercise 10.6

> The U.S. Constitution is a document that lists the philosophy and ideals of the United States. The Constitution includes amendments, which add to or change what is in it. The first Amendment of the U.S. Constitution promises that all people are free to speak. The government added this amendment to the Constitution in 1789, and it is still a part of the Constitution today. It is common, however, for people to question the limits of this amendment. Some people say anything at any time and use the Constitution for protection.

a. What is your opinion of this amendment?

_____

_____

_____

b. Words that are acceptable to one person might be offensive to another. If a person has the freedom to say anything, who can decide when this person has said too much?

_____

_____

_____

_____

c. In the United States, a person in an airport who jokes about having a bomb in his or her suitcase can be arrested, even if there is nothing dangerous in the luggage. What is your opinion of this?

_____

_____

_____

_____

d. In the United States, if a person makes a statement that he or she is going to kill the president and someone with legal authority hears that statement, then the person can be arrested. Do you think that this is acceptable? Why or why not?

_____

_____

_____

_____

Exercise 10.7

Now work in small groups to discuss your answers to exercise 10.6. Be sure to take turns expressing your opinions and to give reasons to support your ideas.

Exercise 10.8

Read the situation involving a student who fought to defend her right to express her opinions.

A 15-year-old high school student in Concord, North Carolina, wore a Confederate* battle flag patch on her backpack. The soldiers in the South flew the Confederate flag during the Civil War in the United States. At first, the flag represented southern history and pride, but now it often represents racism. The student, Katie Knight, refused to take the patch off her backpack. She said that she should be allowed to be proud of her history.

In an earlier case in 1969, the U.S. Supreme Court ruled that "school officials cannot censor student expression unless the expression creates a substantial disruption . . . [of] the educational process or violates the rights of others," which means that schools can't tell students what to say, think, or wear if it doesn't bother anyone or make trouble in school.

---

*The Confederacy refers to the thirteen southern states that separated from the United States in the 1860s. The war that followed is known as the Civil War or the War between the States.

School superintendent Harold Winkler agreed with the school's principal, who told the student not to wear the patch. Winkler believes that "the right of students to express [their opinions] at school is limited by the rights of all to be able to learn in a safe, nonthreatening environment." In other words, he respects Katie Knight's freedom, but he also respects the freedom of the other students.

Exercise 10.9

If you were a public official in North Carolina, what would you decide? Should the student be able to wear whatever she likes? Give reasons for your answer.

_____

_____

_____

_____

_____

_____

_____

Exercise 10.10

An 18-year-old student in Providence, Rhode Island, was sent home from school because he was wearing a shirt with the numbers 666 on it. Some people believe these numbers refer to Satan and satanic worship. The Rhode Island Department of Education ruled that the school was wrong to do this because, according to the American Civil Liberties Union, an organization that protects people's civil rights, "The school's dress [rules] . . . violated free-speech rights."

Do you agree with the Department of Education's decision? Give reasons for your answer.

_____

_____

_____

_____

_____

Do you think it is more acceptable to wear clothes that can express racial prejudice than to wear clothes that can express devil worship? _____

Why or why not? _____

_____

_____

_____

_____

Do either of these things hurt other people? _____

_____

_____

_____

_____

Exercise 10.11

Read this situation involving freedom of speech and government rights.

In September 1999, New York City mayor Rudolph Giuliani threatened to remove city financial support from an exhibit in the Brooklyn Museum of Art. The mayor said the contents of some of the exhibits were "sick" and offensive to Catholics. Specifically, the mayor disliked the work of Chris Ofili, a British artist with Nigerian roots. Ofili's work *The Holy Virgin Mary* shows the Virgin Mary, an important figure in the Catholic religion, covered with cow feces, which Ofili used to represent his African roots.

In a case decided in 1998, the Supreme Court warned that the power of the government to give money cannot be used to punish artists who create and show unpopular work and that the government must remain neutral.

Exercise 10.12

Which side do you agree with in this situation? Give reasons for your answer.

_____

_____

_____

_____

_____

_____

Exercise 10.13

Work in small groups. Discuss your decision and your reasons. See communication activity 59 to find out the outcome of this controversy.

Language Review

This review has two parts. The directions for each part are the same. Match the vocabulary items from the left column with their definitions in the right column.

Part a

Vocabulary	*Definition*
___ 1. allowed	a. a train that runs underground
___ 2. disturb	b. permitted; let
___ 3. race	c. a disagreement
___ 4. background	d. bother; interrupt
___ 5. financial	e. slang term for *homosexual*
___ 6. controversy	f. history
___ 7. subway	g. a group of people who share similar nationality and often physical characteristics
___ 8. queer	h. relating to money

Part b

Vocabulary	*Definition*
___ 1. commissioner	a. safe; not likely to hurt someone
___ 2. amendment	b. solid waste from animals and humans
___ 3. patch	c. manager; administrative official
___ 4. nonthreatening	d. something that causes anger
___ 5. prejudice	e. improvement; correction; change
___ 6. worship	f. a piece of cloth usually worn on clothing
___ 7. offensive	g. admire or idolize, usually relating to religion
___ 8. feces	h. a preformed negative opinion of someone that is not based on the person as an individual

Finish the Story:
The Mysterious Robbery

Exercise 11.1

Read the following true story.

> In May, 1995 in Mount Juliet, Tennessee, something very strange happened to Shirley and Rick Wheeler. They went to the front of their house and saw that something was missing. Thieves stole something from the Wheelers that is necessary, large, and difficult to replace. Of course, the Wheelers were very, very surprised.

Exercise 11.2

Think about the situation described in exercise 11.1 and then think of three possible answers for this question: What did the thieves take from the Wheelers? Write your answers here.

_____

_____

_____

_____

_____

Exercise 11.3

Discuss your answers in small groups. The group should choose its best answer to exercise 11.2 and tell it to the class. Other students should give reasons why they agree or disagree with the answer or ask questions to get more information.

Exercise 11.4

Hot or Cold?

A panel of "experts" should be chosen from the class. Perhaps one person from each of the groups can be chosen. The panel should sit in a row of chairs at the front of the room. Only the panel members should read communication activity 50 to find out what the thieves stole. The other students take turns making statements about what they think happened. The panel members can use "hot" or "cold" to say if the students are far from the real answer or close to the real answer. If no progress is being made, the judges (or teacher) may decide to give a few clues to help out the guessers.

Here are some helpful expressions for playing "Hot or Cold."

"You're hot."	=	"You almost have the right answer."
"You're warm."	=	"You're near the answer."
"You're cold."	=	"You are not near the answer at all."
"You're getting warmer."	=	That is a better answer. You're starting to get the right idea."
"You're getting colder."	=	"You're going away from the answer."

Useful language:
Did the thieves . . . ?
Was the thing a . . . ?
Did they need the thing for . . . ?
How much money did the thing cost?

Language Review

Read the key word or phrase (in bold) in the left column. Circle the letter of the choice that is related to the key word or phrase.

1. **missing**   a. not far   b. not here   c. sad

2. **a thief**   a. steal   b. work   c. drive

3. **warm**   a. hot   b. freeze   c. cost

4. **replace**   a. find another   b. find nothing   c. find information

5. **gravel**   a. small birds   b. small trees   c. small rocks

6. **happen**   a. occur   b. surprise   c. report

7. **large**   a. wide   b. left   c. big

8. **stole**   a. gave something   b. ate something   c. took something

9. **necessary**   a. listen   b. maybe   c. need

10. **of course**   a. only   b. surely   c. perhaps

Be sure to visit <www.press.umich.edu/esl> for ideas on related Web sites, videos, and other activities.

UNIT 12

Animal Vocabulary

When in Rome, do as the Romans do.

Exercise 12.1

"When in Rome, do as the Romans do" is an expression about understanding another culture. Every culture has certain ideas about some animals. For example, an animal may represent courage or bravery. However, that same animal might represent something very different in another culture.

Here is a multiple-choice quiz to see how well you know what people in the United States and Canada think of these animals. Write the letter of the correct answer on the line and then write one sentence explaining your choice.

1. I'm so hungry that I could eat _____.
   (= I'm very hungry.)
   a. a bear   b. a horse   c. a snake

A bear

   reason: _____

   _____

2. He eats like _____. (= He eats very little.)
   a. a bird   b. a cat   c. a donkey

   reason: _____

   _____

3. You're _____. (= You're afraid.)
   a. an ant   b. a chicken   c. a monkey

   reason: _____

   _____

A donkey

4. Proverb: Curiosity killed the _____. (We think this animal is very inquisitive.)
   a. cat   b. giraffe   c. turtle

   reason: _____

   _____

5. You have the memory of _____. (= You have a good memory.)
   a. an elephant   b. a horse   c. an ostrich

   reason: _____

   _____

   _____

An ostrich

6. He is _____ in sheep's clothing. (= He is someone that you cannot trust.)
   a. a deer   b. a monkey   c. a wolf

   reason: _____

   _____

7. Which of these animals is thought to be brave, full of courage?
   a. a duck   b. a lion   c. a tiger

   reason: _____

   _____

8. Which of these animals is thought to be wise, intelligent?
   a. a gorilla   b. a kangaroo   c. an owl

   reason: _____

   _____

   An owl

9. Which of these animals is called "man's best friend"?
   a. a dog   b. a horse   c. a pig

   reason: _____

   _____

10. Which of these animals is thought to be playful and
    full of adventure?
    a. a monkey   b. a tiger   c. a whale

    reason: _____

    _____

    A whale

Exercise 12.2

After you finish exercise 12.1, work in pairs or small groups of three or four students to compare your answers. Check the questions one by one. Students should take turns saying what they wrote for each question and why.

When you have finished discussing your possible meanings, check communication activity 57 for the answers.

Which three questions were missed by the most students in your pair or group? __, __, __

Exercise 12.3

Look at this list of animals. What do these animals represent in your native culture? Are any of these animals positive? Are any of them negative? Is this the same in English?

Animal	+ / −	Reason
Bear	—	_____
Bee	—	_____

Animal	+ / −	Reason
Bird	—	_____
Cat	—	_____
Chicken	—	_____
Cow	—	_____
Crow	—	_____
Dog	—	_____
Donkey	—	_____
Dove	—	_____
Duck	—	_____
Eagle	—	_____
Fox	—	_____
Frog	—	_____
Goat	—	_____
Goose	—	_____
Horse	—	_____
Lion	—	_____
Mouse	—	_____
Owl	—	_____
Pig	—	_____
Sheep	—	_____
Snake	—	_____
Spider	—	_____
Turkey	—	_____
Wolf	—	_____

Exercise 12.4

Work in small groups (three to five students is best). Compare your answers for the animals in exercise 12.3. When you finish, compare your group's answers with those of other groups in your class. Which ones are similar? Which ones are different?

Exercise 12.5

What about animals in your own language/culture? Write the names of five animals on the lines on the left. Then write what each animal symbolizes for you.

Animal	What does the animal represent?
snake	bad, evil, not trusted
1.	
2.	
3.	
4.	
5.	

Exercise 12.6

Work in pairs or small groups. Compare your answers. What is similar? What is different? What answers are the most surprising to you?

Exercise 12.7

Expressions with Animal Words

Fill in the blanks with the animal names in the box. You may have to change the ending of a word to make it fit.

butterflies	sheep	cat	cats	snake	ants
horse	horse	wolf	dogs	monkey	frog

1. It's raining _____ and _____. (= It's raining very hard.)

2. He is a _____ in _____'s clothing. (= He appears to be nice, but he isn't.)

3. Curiosity killed the _____.

4. I'm so hungry that I could eat a _____. (= I'm very hungry.)

5. He's a _____ in the grass. (= He is someone that you cannot trust.)

6. They are _____ing around. (= They're playing. They're not working seriously.)

7. They are _____ing around. (= They're playing. They're not working seriously.)

8. I have a _____ in my throat. (= I'm having problems speaking.)

9. I have _____ in my stomach. (= I'm very nervous about something.)

10. She has _____ in her pants. (= She can't sit still. She has to be busy.)

Exercise 12.8

Now compare answers with another student. What are your reasons for the answers that you wrote? When you have finished discussing the animal word answers, check communication activity 58 for the answers.

Exercise 12.9

What sounds do animals make in your native language or another language you know? What sounds do these animals make in English? Here are some animals and their sounds in English. Write the sounds from another language.

Animal	English Sound	Another Language
1. cat	meow	_____
2. dog	bowwow, woof	_____
3. bird	chirp chirp	_____
4. cow	moo	_____
5. rooster	cock-a-doodle-doo	_____
6. frog	ribbit	_____

Exercise 12.10

Now share your answers from exercise 12.9. Feel free to add other animals for which you know the pronunciation of the natural sounds. Which ones are surprises to you? Why?

Language Review

Read the key word or phrase (in bold) in the left column. Circle the letter of the choice that is related to the key word or phrase.

1. **brave**   a. not stupid   b. not afraid   c. not angry

2. **curious**   a. interested   b. surprised   c. frightened

3. **inquisitive**   a. information   b. preparation   c. relaxation

4. **wise**   a. intelligent   b. hungry   c. bored

5. **adventure**   a. dull time   b. exciting time   c. sad time

6. **playful**   a. makes noise   b. wants to watch sports   c. likes to play

7. **symbolizes**   a. represents   b. understands   c. teaches

8. **trust**   a. request   b. believe   c. know

9. **an ant**   a. big   b. medium   c. little

10. **memory**   a. cement   b. December   c. remember

A Serious Post Office Mistake

Ben Pickett:
the stamp with a mistake

Bill Pickett:
the correct stamp

Exercise 13.1

A unique part of the history of the United States is the period often called The Wild West. There were many famous, important people who lived during that time. Some of the important people during this time were

Buffalo Bill	Annie Oakley
Wyatt Earp	Bill Pickett
Wild Bill Hickok	Calamity Jane

Consult an encyclopedia or the Internet. Find out some important facts about one of these people. (1) What was the person's real name? (2) What was the person's background? (3) When was the person born? (4) Why is the person famous today?

_____

_____

_____

_____

_____

_____

_____

_____

_____

_____

_____

_____

_____

_____

_____

Exercise 13.2

Practice making an oral presentation of approximately three minutes about the person that you chose in exercise 13.1. Then give your presentation to a small group or to the class. When you present, pronounce clearly and loudly so that everyone can understand what you are saying. If there is something that you do not understand when someone else presents, ask questions at the end of the presentation.

Exercise 13.3

One aspect of American history that is unique is the development of the American West. In 1994, the U.S. Postal Service designed a special sheet of 20 stamps to honor famous people connected with the West. This series included "Buffalo Bill" Cody, Wyatt Earp, Annie Oakley, and Bill Pickett.

After the sheets of stamps had been printed (but still two months before the sales date), a problem was discovered with the picture of Bill Pickett. Family members and historians said that the man in the stamp was not Bill Pickett. In fact, it was Ben Pickett, Bill's brother.

The postmaster general, Marvin T. Runyon, faced a unique dilemma. What should he do? Ben Pickett was not a famous character in the American West, but in reality very few people would notice the error. In addition, there was the issue of cost. Though stamps are usually printed one stamp per sheet, in this case all 20 stamps were printed on the same sheet. Thus, it was not possible to just reprint the sheets of the one stamp that had an error. It would be necessary to reprint all the sheets of the whole series. The stamps had already been distributed but had not gone on sale yet. Reprinting this sheet of stamps would cost over a million dollars ($1,200,000 to be exact).

If you were the postmaster, what would you do? Try to think of three possible solutions to this special problem. Write down your answers on the lines.

1. _____

   _____

2. _____

   _____

3. _____

   _____

Exercise 13.4

a. Now work in pairs or small groups. Compare answers for exercise 13.3 with the other students. Discuss the pros and cons of each suggestion.

b. What do you think Postmaster Runyon finally decided to do? Write your answer here.

_____

_____

_____

_____

c. Now look at communication activity 15 to find out what the postmaster did.

Language Review

Read the key word (in bold) in the left column. Circle the letter of the choice that is related to the key word.

1. **unique**	a. common	b. unusual	c. sometimes
2. **famous**	a. well-known	b. well-liked	c. well-built
3. **during**	a. within the room	b. within the time	c. within the rules
4. **consult**	a. belong to	b. refer to	c. give to
5. **encyclopedia**	a. religious book	b. reference book	c. history book
6. **background**	a. history	b. future	c. present
7. **aspect**	a. game	b. part	c. problem
8. **designed**	a. damaged	b. asked	c. created
9. **honor**	a. show controversy	b. show anger	c. show respect
10. **historians**	a. study science	b. study history	c. study mathematics
11. **dilemma**	a. problem	b. solution	c. partner
12. **error**	a. reward	b. penalty	c. mistake

13. **issue**   a. ink   b. design   c. publish

14. **reprint**   a. print once   b. print again   c. print badly

15. **series**   a. one   b. a pair   c. a group

16. **distributed** a. gave   b. collected   c. wrote

17. **pros**   a. disadvantages   b. benefits   c. experience

18. **cons**   a. education   b. disadvantages   c. benefits

19. **mistake**   a. topic   b. error   c. background

20. **notice**   a. see   b. buy   c. stay

"Three Hots and a Cot": Prison Conditions and Prisoners' Rights

Exercise 14.1

Look at the title of this unit. What do you think it means? Write your opinion on the lines below. Be sure to give reasons for your answer. (*Hint:* A cot is a small portable bed. See the illustration.)

A cot

_____

_____

_____

_____

Exercise 14.2

Work in small groups.

a. Discuss your responses to the question in exercise 14.1.
b. When you finish, turn to communication activity 43 to read the meaning of this phrase.
c. What is your response to this explanation? Were you surprised by what you read? Did it frighten you? Did it disappoint you? With your group, discuss your responses to the explanation of the title of this unit.

Exercise 14.3

Read the statements below and decide whether you agree or disagree with them. Circle *A* if you agree and *D* if you disagree. Then explain your answers on the lines provided.

1. A   D   The purpose of a prison is to punish criminals.

   _____

   _____

2. A   D   The purpose of a prison is to rehabilitate criminals.

   _____

   _____

3. A   D   Prisoners should be treated with respect.

   _____

   _____

4. A   D   Prisoners should receive free health care, including medicine and operations, while in prison.

   _____

   _____

5. A   D   Prisons should have places for prisoners to exercise and lift
             weights.

_____

_____

6. A   D   A convicted murderer should live in an air-conditioned prison.

_____

_____

7. A   D   Prisoners should be able to receive visits from their family mem-
             bers.

_____

_____

8. A   D   Prisoners should receive an education while they are in prison
             (e.g., their high school or university education).

_____

_____

Exercise 14.4

Read the following excerpts from an article outlining a protest in a Texas prison.

> Some death-row inmates are refusing meals because they disagree
> with the way they are living at the Terrell Unit of the Texas Department
> of Criminal Justice in Livingston, Texas. They are complaining because
> they have no television. Also, they are unhappy because they can no
> longer work and earn money for themselves.
>
> The prisoners complain about their living environment, too. They
> are angry because they have solid steel doors and not the usual prison
> bars, and they are unhappy because they spend their recreation and
> relaxation time alone and not with other prisoners.
>
> Gloria Rubac, a representative for the Texas Death Penalty Abolition
> Movement, supports the inmates' protest. She believes that the lack of

human contact many death-row inmates experience may cause them to "go [crazy] before they're ever executed just because of the isolation." While she understands that most people in her state support the death penalty, Rubac hopes that "they don't support [hurting people unnecessarily] until they're executed."

Exercise 14.5

Write your reaction to the information in exercise 14.4. Be sure to give reasons for your answer.

_____

_____

_____

_____

_____

Exercise 14.6

Work in small groups. Discuss your answers to exercise 14.5.

Exercise 14.7

Read the statements below and decide if you think each situation is acceptable or unacceptable. Circle *A* for acceptable and *U* for unacceptable. Then explain your answers on the lines provided.

1. A   U   Some of the most common causes of death in prison are disease, lack of medical care, too many people, poor food, and unclean conditions.

_____

_____

2. A U   In some Venezuelan prisons, there is one guard for every 150
           prisoners.

_____

_____

3. A U   Powerful inmates in some prisons in Colombia, India, and
           Mexico enjoy cellular phones, delicious food, and comfortable
           rooms.

_____

_____

4. A U   In many prisons that are full (have no room for additional pris-
           oners), the inmates don't have enough space to stretch or move
           around.

_____

_____

5. A U   In some prisons, inmates must wear chains around their ankles,
           which makes walking very painful.

_____

_____

Exercise 14.8

Work in small groups. Discuss your responses to exercise 14.7.

Exercise 14.9

Read the information about a topic that is becoming more and more controversial in the United States.

As of March 29, 2000, ex-convicts in 11 of the United States automatically and permanently lose their right to participate in elections. The states that permanently prohibit all ex-convicts from voting are Alabama, Delaware, Florida, Iowa, Kentucky, Mississippi, Nevada, New Mexico, Tennessee, Virginia, and Wyoming. The result is that 1.4 million ex-prisoners cannot vote.

People who support this law offer several reasons why they agree with it. Stanford law professor Pamela Karlan argues that "somebody serving 20 years in an . . . Illinois prison [should not choose] the mayor of Chicago, where he no longer lives." In addition, another fear is that inmates who vote in their current neighborhoods (where the jails are) greatly affect the small town in which their prison is located.

Other people who support this law believe that criminals do not make good decisions for themselves. In addition, they feel that some criminals may vote for weak law enforcement, and they want to protect the government from this.

People who disagree with the law suggest that, while punishment is one function of the criminal justice system, rehabilitation is another important goal. People who disagree with the law fear that "it tells the [criminal] that no matter what he does, he can never fully [come back to] the community he [hurt]." They believe that the law doesn't help criminals come back into society; it keeps them out of society forever.

Exercise 14.10

What is your position on banning prisoners and ex-convicts from voting? Write your opinion on the lines below. Be sure to give reasons for your answer.

_____

_____

_____

_____

Exercise 14.11

Work in small groups. Discuss your response to exercise 14.10.

Exercise 14.12

Role Play

Scene: The Board of County Commissioners is meeting to discuss prison conditions. You should attend the meeting and try to encourage the board members to agree with your position. Possible roles: a convicted felon, a prison guard, a crime victim, a civil rights activist, board members.

Your role:

_____

Your position on this issue:

_____

_____

_____

_____

_____

_____

_____

 **Language Review**

Read the key word or phrase (in bold) in the left column. Circle the letter of the choice that is related to the key word or phrase.

1. **purpose**   a. difference   b. reason   c. problem

2. **convict**   a. prisoner   b. teacher   c. driver

3. **cot**   a. past of *catch*   b. warm   c. a portable bed

4. **executed**   a. killed   b. carried out   c. better than good

5. **refusing**   a. saying no   b. saying yes   c. saying please

6. **inmates**   a. visitors   b. prisoners   c. partners

7. **complain about**   a. a great dinner   b. a pretty baby   c. a bad situation

8. **recreation**   a. work   b. play   c. study

9. **supports**   a. agrees with   b. talks to   c. finds out

10. **protest**   a. strongly want   b. strongly work   c. strongly disagree

11. **isolation**   a. time with friends   b. time alone   c. time in cold weather

12. **punish**   a. paint   b. put in prison   c. play sports with

13. **rehabilitate**   a. visit many times   b. put in danger again   c. help and make better

14. **lack of**   a. not enough   b. not correct   c. not serious

15. **permanently** a. at times   b. temporary   c. forever

16. **prohibit**   a. allow   b. forbid   c. accept

17. **current**   a. past   b. present   c. future

18. **function**   a. job   b. game   c. mistake

19. **refuse**   a. not accept   b. not understand   c. not connect

20. **due to**   a. although   b. because   c. without

Put the Story Together:
The Cat and the Tree

Exercise 15.1

Can you guess what happened? Work in groups of 10.* Each student will have a piece of a story. Try to put the story together.

Step 1. Each student should look at one of these communication activities: 1, 6, 11, 16, 21, 26, 31, 36, 41, 46.

---

*If there are extra students, these students should be judges. The judges should listen to the story lines and decide if the 10 students have put themselves in the correct order or not. Conversely, if there are not 10 students, the teacher should participate, and perhaps one or two of the lines could be copied on a sheet of paper that could be placed on the floor in the correct position within the story. (See step 4.)

Step 2. Write your activity number in the box and write your sentence on the lines.

⬚ _____

_____

Step 3. You have one minute to read and memorize your piece of the story. You do not have to use the exact same words, but you need to express the same idea.

Step 4. The 10 students should stand up and put themselves (i.e., their pieces of the story) in order by taking turns saying (not reading) their lines aloud.

Exercise 15.2

For homework, write another strip story like the one in exercise 15.1. Do not have more than 10 lines; fewer lines are OK if you have a smaller class. Try to have a funny ending. Write one copy of your story on a sheet of paper and make another copy that you will cut up into strips to give to students.

Exercise 15.3

In some countries, it is common for people to have dogs, cats, birds, and fish live in their houses with them. The people feed them and play with them. Sometimes people love their pets almost as much as they love their families. Does this happen in your country? Do you keep animals in your house? What kinds of animals can you have as pets? What kinds of names do you give to your pets? Give examples. Write your answers on the lines. Be sure to give reasons for your answers.

_____

_____

_____

_____

_____

_____

Exercise 15.4

Work in small groups. Discuss your answers to the questions in exercise 15.3.

 **Language Review**

Match the vocabulary items in the left column with their definitions in the right column.

Vocabulary	*Definition*
___ 1. return	a. an area of a building or business
___ 2. found	b. search, try to find
___ 3. department	c. come back; bring back
___ 4. upset	d. past tense of *find*
___ 5. look for	e. very angry, sad, or worried
___ 6. outside	f. morning food
___ 7. dead	g. put
___ 8. sir	h. polite name used when speaking to a man
___ 9. breakfast	i. not inside
___ 10. place	j. not alive

Group Speaking Puzzle: Travel

Exercise 16.1

Work in groups of three. Student A should look at communication activity 10; student B, 33; and student C, 53. Each of these communication activities contains clues to some of the answers to the crossword puzzle.

Step 1. Use the clues in your communication activity to solve the puzzle.

Step 2. When you have used all your clues, you and your two partners should ask each other for clues about the answers that you do not know. Do not look at your partners' communication activities during this step. It is okay to use the clues from the communication activities, but you may not refer to the communication activities themselves. Try to make up your own descriptions for the answers whenever possible. Do not tell the answers directly to anyone and do not spell any of the letters of the answers.

Exercise 16.2

After you finish the puzzle, work in small groups. Discuss your answers to these questions.

1. What do you know about number 6 across? Has anyone in your group traveled there before?
2. Number 12 across is the noun for the verb *fly.* Describe a time that you were on a flight that had any kind of problems (bad weather, delays at the airport, etc.). What happened? What did you do?

3. Number 14 down is something that you use when you go camping. Did you ever go camping? How often do you usually go camping? Where do you go? Do you know how to set up a tent quickly?

4. Number 17 across is a special fee or money that we all have to pay. How much is the sales tax where you live? Can you think of a place that has a higher sales tax? What about a place that has a lower sales tax?

5. Number 8 across is *art*. What is your favorite kind of art? Do you have a favorite painter or painting? How many famous art museums have you visited?

6. Number 1 down is a country in Eastern Europe. What do you know about this country?

7. Number 19 across is a small body of water, a bay. Can you think of other names of bodies of water in English?

8. Number 7 down is *relax*. What is your favorite or most common way to relax?

 Language Review

Read the key word or phrase (in bold) in the left column. Circle the letter of the choice that is related to the key word or phrase.

1. **bay**   a. water   b. country   c. famous

2. **relax**   a. no food   b. no work   c. no sports

3. **flight**   a. column   b. favorite   c. airplane

4. **taxi**   a. cab   b. money   c. two

5. **tax**   a. cab   b. money   c. two

6. **good time**   a. aisle   b. across   c. fun

7. **profession**   a. believe   b. mountain   c. teacher

8. **tent**   a. for sleeping   b. for working   c. for cooking

9. **temporary**   a. short time   b. no money   c. a lot of people

10. **museum**   a. tree   b. color   c. art

11. **aisle**   a. in a plane   b. in a desk   c. in a museum

12. **clue**   a. some people   b. some money   c. some help

13. **minus**   a. $5 + 2 = 7$ b. $5 \times 2 = 10$ c. $5 - 2 = 3$

14. **food**   a. eat   b. drink   c. send

15. **purple**   a. size   b. color   c. sound

16. **opposite**   a. different   b. interesting   c. appropriate

17. **ride**   a. in a car   b. on a chair   c. near a fish

18. **make up**   a. create   b. tell   c. travel

Double Vision: Cloning

sheep 1   sheep 1 again

Exercise 17.1

Read this true story of a controversial scientific success story and then answer the questions that follow.

> In February 1997, scientists at the Roslin Institute in Roslin, Midlothian, the United Kingdom, published an article in *Nature*. The article informed the public of their shared success with PPL Therapeutics. Working together, the Roslin Institute and PPL Therapeutics cloned a sheep from fetal and adult cells.
>
> Dr. Ian Wilmut and his team of scientists from the Roslin Institute cloned Dolly the sheep. As reported in *Time* magazine, biologically, Dolly does not simply look similar to her biological mother; she is a copy of her mother, or in other words, her mother's identical twin.

1. What is one good thing about what you just read? _____

_____

_____

_____

2. What is one bad thing about what you just read? _____

_____

_____

_____

3. What is your opinion of the experiment described? _____

_____

_____

_____

Exercise 17.2

Work in small groups. Discuss your answers to exercise 17.1.

Exercise 17.3

Read the following statements and indicate your reactions by circling 1 if you *agree strongly*, 2 if you *agree somewhat*, 3 if you are *not sure*, 4 if you *disagree somewhat*, and 5 if you *disagree strongly*. Then write your opinions about these statements. Be sure to include one or two reasons to explain your opinions.

a. 1   2   3   4   5   There are benefits to cloning animals.

_____

_____

b. 1 2 3 4 5 It is acceptable to clone animals for the purpose of feeding people.

_____

_____

c. 1 2 3 4 5 Cloning an animal raises serious questions of what is right and wrong.

_____

_____

d. 1 2 3 4 5 It is a good idea to clone endangered animals to save them from extinction.

_____

_____

e. 1 2 3 4 5 It is acceptable to clone an animal and use it for research that can someday help to cure human diseases.

_____

_____

Exercise 17.4

Work in groups to discuss your responses to the statements in exercise 17.3.

Exercise 17.5

Write your reactions to the following statements.

1. If you're cloning someone to replace a child who died, then you might love the new child especially dearly. However, the new child might not like the reason that it was born.

_____

_____

_____

2. Cloning humans can change relationships between parents and children and husbands and wives.

_____

_____

_____

3. Some parents may use cloning because they want to have a child who looks like someone in the family.

_____

_____

_____

4. Parents whose child has a terminal illness could use cloning to copy their dying child.

_____

_____

_____

5. Some people think cloning is similar to abortion because many fetuses would die because of it.

_____

_____

_____

6. Cloning humans may soon be so simple that no laws can stop it.

_____

_____

_____

7. In the future, a sample of a person's blood may give you all the biological information necessary to make a copy of that person without the person knowing it.

Exercise 17.6

Work in groups to discuss your responses to the statements in exercise 17.5.

Exercise 17.7

Read the following topic for consideration.

> Theorists and researchers often consider the question of nature versus nurture, that is, whether people grow in a certain way because of biology or because of their environments. This creates an interesting question about cloning: Will the cloned person and his or her clone be exactly the same or only similar? Some theorists believe that clones are exactly the same, but others believe that biology alone does not make people but that their life experiences and environment create them.

Exercise 17.8

What is your opinion on the subject of nature versus nurture? Which one do you think is more important for how a person turns out to be as an adult? Write your response here.

_____

_____

_____

_____

Exercise 17.9

Work in small groups. Discuss your answers to exercise 17.8.

 **Language Review**

This review has two parts. The directions for each part are the same. Match the vocabulary items in the left column with their definitions in the right column.

Part a

Vocabulary	*Definition*
___ 1. controversial	a. All animals in the species are dead.
___ 2. informed	b. something that people disagree about
___ 3. fetal	c. an advantage; a good thing
___ 4. identical	d. told; gave information
___ 5. benefit	e. exactly the same
___ 6. extinct	f. relating to an unborn baby
___ 7. similar	g. almost the same
___ 8. share	h. give things to someone
___ 9. twin	i. one of two babies born at the same time
___ 10. success	j. something with very good results

Part b

Vocabulary	Definition
___ 1. cure	a. think about
___ 2. terminal	b. an example; a part of; a piece of
___ 3. an abortion	c. remove an illness forever
___ 4. a sample	d. an illness that can kill a person; resulting in death
___ 5. consider	e. take care of; help grow
___ 6. nurture	f. the intentional ending of a pregnancy
___ 7. feed	g. not correct
___ 8. wrong	h. a story in a newspaper or magazine
___ 9. an article	i. when a person is sick
___ 10. an illness	j. give food to

Put the Story Together: I Don't Want to Go to School

Exercise 18.1

Can you guess what happened? Work in groups of eight.* Each student will have a piece of a story. Try to put the story together.

Step 1. Each student should look at one of these communication activities: 2, 9, 17, 24, 32, 39, 45, 51.

Step 2. Write your activity number in the box and write your sentence on the lines.

*If there are extra students, these students should be judges. The judges should listen to the story lines and decide if the eight students have put themselves in the correct order or not. Conversely, if there are not eight students, the teacher should participate, and perhaps one or two of the lines could be copied on a sheet of paper that could be placed on the floor in the correct position within the story. (See step 4.)

Step 3.　You have one minute to read and memorize your piece of the story. You do not have to use the exact same words, but you need to express the same idea.

Step 4.　The eight students should stand up and put themselves (i.e., their pieces of the story) in order by taking turns saying (not reading) their lines aloud.

Exercise 18.2

For homework, write another strip story like the one in exercise 18.1. Do not have more than 10 lines; fewer lines are OK if you have a smaller class. Try to have a funny ending. Write one copy of your story on a sheet of paper and make another copy that you will cut up into strips to give to students.

Exercise 18.3

In the United States, it is not common for children to live with their parents after they have their own jobs. What do you think of this? Write your opinion on the lines.

_____

_____

_____

_____

_____

When you were a child, how did you feel about going to school? Were you happy about it, or did you dislike it? Why? Give specific reasons.

_____

_____

_____

_____

_____

Exercise 18.4

Work in small groups. Discuss your answers to the questions in exercise 18.3.

 **Language Review**

Match the vocabulary items in the left column with their definitions in the right column.

Vocabulary	*Definition*
___ 1. principal	a. try to remember something
___ 2. common	b. person who manages a school
___ 3. memorize	c. purpose; why we do things
___ 4. reason	d. usual; ordinary
___ 5. hate	e. dislike strongly
___ 6. kid	f. an informal (slang) word for *child*
___ 7. number one	g. the second reason for something
___ 8. wake up	h. stop sleeping
___ 9. early	i. not late
___ 10. number two	j. the first reason for something

A School for Men Only?

Who can enter the military?

Exercise 19.1

Read this short passage regarding a famous military school in South Carolina.

> The Citadel is a military college that the state of South Carolina started in the city of Charleston in 1842. It is a state-supported school, which means that it receives money from the government (from taxpayers).
>
> In 1993, something interesting happened because of one of the people who applied to be a new student at the college. Shannon Faulkner filled out all of her application papers. She also organized her high school information, including her transcripts. Before she submitted her paperwork, she took out all of the references to the fact that she

is a woman. (For example, she took out *she* in the comments that people had written about her.) Why did Shannon Faulkner do this? She did this because the Citadel had a policy that would not permit female students to apply to the college.

The Citadel reviewed her application and then rejected it when the school officials learned that she was a woman. She sued the school for the right of admission, claiming that the school had violated her equal-rights protection. In other words, she sued on the grounds of sexual or gender discrimination.

In its defense, the school officials said that the single-gender admission policy was part of the school's history that made the school special. The officials said that the school had a "justified single-gender admissions policy that has defined its institutional mission" and student body since its founding. Furthermore, the officials said that a woman attending classes would cause irreparable harm "because a male environment is essential to the Citadel's overall educational mission."

Exercise 19.2

What is your reaction to this decision? If you were the judge or jury, what would you say? Do you agree with the school officials or with Shannon? Would you order the school officials to permit Shannon to enter the school? Be sure to give several specific reasons when you explain your opinion.

_____

_____

_____

_____

_____

_____

Exercise 19.3

Work in small groups. Discuss your answers to exercise 19.2. As you listen to everyone, write down one reason that you hear that supports allowing women to attend the school and one reason that supports not allowing women to attend the school. Make sure these reasons are different from your own reason.

One reason to allow female students at the Citadel: _____

_____

_____

One reason NOT to allow female students at the Citadel: _____

_____

_____

Exercise 19.4

This case eventually reached the Supreme Court of the United States. If you were one of the judges, would you order the school official to let Shannon enter the school? _____ After all the discussion in this unit, have you changed your mind? _____ Read communication activity 18 to find out what the Supreme Court decided.

Exercise 19.5

Some research studies show that students have better grades in school when they study in boys-only or girls-only schools. For this exercise and the discussion in exercise 19.6, there is no communication activity giving an expert answer. These exercises use only the ideas of the people in your class. Make a list of the advantages of being in a single-gender school and another list of the advantages of being in a mixed-gender school.

	Advantages of Being in a Single-Gender School	*Advantages of Being in a Mixed-Gender School*
1.	_____	_____
	_____	_____
	_____	_____

	Advantages of Being in a Single-Gender School	*Advantages of Being in a Mixed-Gender School*
2.	_____	_____
	_____	_____
	_____	_____
3.	_____	_____
	_____	_____
	_____	_____
4.	_____	_____
	_____	_____
	_____	_____
5.	_____	_____
	_____	_____
	_____	_____

Exercise 19.6

Work in small groups. Compare your answers for the situations in exercise 19.5.

Exercise 19.7

Role Play

Work in small groups.

Scene: Some of the main players in the Citadel drama are discussing their ideas on this topic. As you can imagine, the ideas are very different from each other. To try to resolve the problem, the people involved have gathered for an honest discussion. Possible participants: the head official at the Citadel, the parent of Shannon Faulkner, Shannon, a man who graduated from the Citadel and whose father and grandfather both graduated from this very traditional school, a teacher who supports mixed-gender classes.

Your role:

_____

Your position on this issue:

_____

_____

_____

_____

_____

_____

_____

_____

 ## Language Review

Read the key word or phrase (in bold) in the left column. Circle the letter of the choice that is related to the key word or phrase.

1. **organized**   a. required   b. put in order

2. **a transcript**   a. a record of grades b. a court for children

3. **submitted**   a. formally requested b. formally gave

4. **policy**   a. a set of rules   b. a set of requests

5. **permit**   a. want   b. allow

6. **rejected**   a. refused   b. reviewed

7. **claiming**   a. saying   b. believing

8. **violated**   a. went against   b. agreed with

9. **gender**   a. race   b. sex

10. **discrimination**   a. unfair treatment   b. unusual treatment

11. **justified**   a. equal   b. right or fair

12. **mission**   a. effort   b. goal

13. **special**   a. not usual   b. not good quality

14. **irreparable**   a. able to be fixed   b. unable to be fixed

15. **jury**   a. people who disagree   b. people who decide

16. **expert**   a. very knowledgeable   b. very different

17. **overall**   a. general   b. excellent

18. **founding**   a. the beginning   b. the middle

19. **harm**   a. bring good luck   b. cause serious problems

20. **furthermore**   a. for this reason   b. in addition

21. **essential**   a. necessary   b. serious

22. **fill out** _____   a. a new car to buy   b. an application for a job

So Who Is the Guilty Criminal?

Exercise 20.1

Read this court case involving a crime in New York City.

In 1984, Bernard McCummings and two other men attacked and robbed Jerome Sandusky, a 72-year-old man, in a New York subway station. They hit and choked him and pinned him to the ground. Fortunately for Sandusky, two policemen were nearby and heard his cries for help. One of the policemen, Manuel Rodriguez, shot Bernard McCummings as he and the other two men were trying to escape from the crime scene. One of the bullets hit McCummings in the spine, and now he cannot walk. He is paralyzed from the chest down.

New York police guidelines state that police can only use guns defensively. They cannot be used to stop a fleeing criminal "unless there is probable cause to believe a felon will use deadly force."

McCummings pleaded guilty to the mugging and served 32 months in jail. (He had previously spent two years in prison on another robbery conviction.)

McCummings then sued the government for $4.3 million. He claimed that excessive force was used and this resulted in his being paralyzed.

Exercise 20.2

If you were the judge in this case, would you decide in favor of McCummings? ___ Write two or three reasons for your decision.

_____

_____

_____

_____

_____

Exercise 20.3

Work in small groups. Discuss your decision and your reasons. When you finish all of the discussion, read the court's decision in communication activity 42.

Exercise 20.4

Work in groups of three or four students. Each person should do one of the four parts (a, b, c, or d).

a. This unit describes how one criminal received an incredibly large amount of money after he committed a crime. Crime is a major problem in the U.S. today. Some people worry that this decision sends the wrong message to criminals. They worry that it tells criminals that crime pays well. Write your thoughts about this here.

_____

_____

_____

_____

_____

_____

b. This unit describes how one criminal received an incredibly large amount of money after he committed a crime. Crime is a major problem for police today. Some people want the police to have more power to be able to stop people fleeing a crime scene, including the ability to shoot a person who is fleeing. Write your thoughts about this here.

_____

_____

_____

_____

_____

c. This unit describes how one criminal received an incredibly large amount of money after he committed a crime. Crime is a major problem for police today. Some people worry that this decision will affect the way that police are able to do their main job, to protect the people. Write your thoughts about this here.

_____

_____

_____

_____

_____

d. This unit describes how one criminal received an incredibly large amount of money after he committed a crime. Crime is a major problem for police today. However, some people are very worried that the police might one day be able to shoot a person who is fleeing a crime scene. They don't want police to have this much power. Write your thoughts about this here.

_____

_____

_____

_____

_____

_____

Exercise 20.5

Work in groups of three or four. Make sure that each person wrote about a different situation in exercise 20.4. Discuss your ideas about the situations and opinions in exercise 20.4. Which opinions sound good to you? Which ones sound very surprising to you?

Exercise 20.6

Role Play

Work in small groups.

Scene: It is the first day of the court appearance for Bernard McCummings, who is suing the government for his injuries. As you can imagine, the participants hold extremely different opinions about this case. Work in groups to role-play this situation. Possible participants: Bernard McCummings; Jerome Sandusky, who was attacked; the policeman who shot McCummings; an elderly woman living in the area who has minded her business all her life but who is now afraid of the crime in her area; one of the men who helped McCummings.

Your role:

Your position on this issue:

_____

_____

_____

_____

_____

_____

_____

 Language Review

This review has two parts. The directions for each part are the same. Match the vocabulary items in the left column with their definitions in the right column.

Part a

Vocabulary	*Definition*
___ 1. attacked	a. permanently unable to move
___ 2. robbed	b. used violent physical or verbal force on someone
___ 3. subway	c. got away from someone or something
___ 4. choked	d. stole someone's possessions
___ 5. escaped	e. in an effort to protect oneself
___ 6. spine	f. an underground train
___ 7. paralyzed	g. backbone
___ 8. defensively	h. grabbed a person's throat to stop the person's breathing

Part b

Vocabulary	*Definition*
—— 1. probable cause	a. number; quantity
—— 2. felon	b. too much; more than enough
—— 3. deadly	c. strong reason to believe someone is dangerous
—— 4. mug	d. run away
—— 5. previously	e. extremely dangerous; resulting in death
—— 6. excessive	f. attack and rob someone
—— 7. incredibly	g. before now
—— 8. amount	h. amazingly; surprisingly
—— 9. flee	i. a person who commits a very serious crime

Animal Rights and Animal Research

No more animal testing???

Exercise 21.1

Read these statements and indicate your reactions by circling 1 if you *agree strongly*, 2 if you *agree somewhat*, 3 if you are *not sure*, 4 if you *disagree somewhat*, and 5 if you *disagree strongly*. Then write your opinions about these statements. Be sure to include one or two reasons to explain your opinions.

a. 1   2   3   4   5   If I need to kill a chicken to have food for myself, I can do it.

_____

_____

b. 1   2   3   4   5   Human life is more valuable than animal life.

_____

_____

c. 1 2 3 4 5   God created animals and humans. They are all equal.

_____

_____

d. 1 2 3 4 5   It is OK to kill cows for beef and for leather.

_____

_____

e. 1 2 3 4 5   We must do everything that we can to end disease in humans even if this means we have to use animals in medical research.

_____

_____

f. 1 2 3 4 5   It is OK to use small animals in research (e.g., mice) but not OK to use larger animals (e.g., monkeys and gorillas).

_____

_____

g. 1 2 3 4 5   It is OK to kill animals for their skins and coats.

_____

_____

h. 1 2 3 4 5   The main goal of medical research is to save human life, and it is OK to use animals in this research.

_____

_____

Exercise 21.2

Work in small groups. Discuss your opinions of the statements in exercise 21.1. Which statement do your opinions differ about the most? ___ Why do you disagree with each other about this statement?

Exercise 21.3

Read the information about an animal research controversy.

> Ten miles off the coast of Java in Indonesia, there is a small island called Tinjil that is the home to several jungle animals, including pythons, brown rats, and monitor lizards. In 1987, scientists put macaque monkeys on the island because they wanted to breed them and create a large population of pure, healthy monkeys. The scientists' goal was to raise the healthy monkeys and then transport them to the United States to be used for AIDS research.
>
> Twice a year, researchers bring about 50 young monkeys to the United States and expose them to a form of the HIV virus that affects monkeys. After the monkeys have gotten the disease, scientists treat them with experimental vaccines. The scientists are searching for a cure for the human HIV virus. So far, a cure has not resulted. Of course, most of these monkeys die after they experience all the pain that any AIDS victim has.

Exercise 21.4

What do you think about this? Write your initial reaction to this situation on the lines below.

_____

_____

_____

_____

_____

_____

_____

_____

Exercise 21.5

Work in small groups. Discuss your answers from exercise 21.4.

Exercise 21.6

There are two separate sides to the animal research controversy. On one side, there are the animal rights activists and philosophers who want to protect animals; on the other side, there are the researchers who want to protect and improve the lives of humans.

You will read six statements that are arguments *for* and *against* animal research. Read each statement. Then put a check mark (✓) to show if the argument is *for* or *against* animal research. Last, write your reactions to the statements on the lines under the statements.

a. _____ for animal research   _____ against animal research
   We have no right to do to mice, rats, and monkeys what we will not do to ourselves.

   _____

   _____

   _____

   _____

b. _____ for animal research   _____ against animal research
   We should not do experiments on animals only because we want to save humans from death and discomfort. It is not the animals' problem that we are sick and dying.

   _____

   _____

   _____

   _____

c. _____ for animal research   _____ against animal research
Good medical research is possible without animals by using alternatives such as computer modeling.

_____

_____

_____

_____

d. _____ for animal research   _____ against animal research
Animals cannot make judgments about what is right and wrong, so they have no freedom.

_____

_____

_____

_____

e. _____ for animal research   _____ against animal research
Two-thirds of all Nobel Prizes for medicine are for discoveries involving animal studies.

_____

_____

_____

_____

f. _____ for animal research   _____ against animal research
There will be no cure, no vaccine, and no progress in the fight against AIDS if we don't use animals for research.

_____

_____

_____

_____

Exercise 21.7

Work in small groups. Discuss your responses to the statements in exercise 21.6.

Exercise 21.8

Role Play

Situation: The government is trying to decide if they should spend $500,000 for AIDS research on animals. Many of these animals will die, but many scientists say this is the best way to do the research because some of the animals have body reactions to AIDS that are very similar to human body reactions to AIDS. Work in groups of four or five. Each person should do one of these communication activities: 8, 19, 30, 40, and 48.

Your role:

_____

Your position on this issue:

_____

_____

_____

_____

_____

_____

_____

_____

Language Review

This review has two parts. The directions for each part are the same. Match the vocabulary items in the left column with their definitions in the right column.

Part a

Vocabulary   *Definition*

___ 1. equal   a. move from one place to another

___ 2. leather   b. the same

___ 3. disease   c. cause to come in contact with

___ 4. coat   d. bring from childhood to adulthood

___ 5. several   e. the skin of a cow

___ 6. breed   f. the hair of an animal

___ 7. raise   g. reproduce animals

___ 8. transport   h. a serious illness

___ 9. expose to   i. greater than two or three but not many

Part b

Vocabulary   *Definition*

___ 1. vaccine   a. political or natural freedom to do things

___ 2. rights   b. medicine that helps to prevent an illness

___ 3. activist   c. onward movement; steady improvement

___ 4. improve   d. choices; options

___ 5. alternatives   e. decisions (by a court)

___ 6. judgments   f. make better

___ 7. progress   g. a person who fights for a cause

Domestic Violence: Who Stops It?

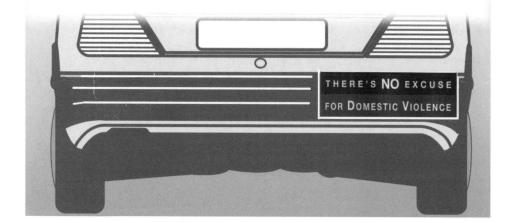

Exercise 22.1

Read the following information about a problem that affects millions of women each year. Then write your reaction on the lines following the passage.

Every year in the United States, two million to four million women are physically assaulted or raped by their husbands, boyfriends, or lovers. Of five thousand women murdered in a single year, more than 70 percent know their attackers. An even more frightening statistic is this one: More than 80 percent of women who leave their abusive spouses and lovers are followed, hit, forced to have sex, or killed. Most women are attacked, sexually assaulted, raped, or murdered in their own homes, and the attacker is the husband or boyfriend. Unfortunately, police don't often prosecute these men because the women refuse to try to convict them.

_____

_____

_____

_____

_____

_____

_____

Exercise 22.2

In small groups, discuss your responses to exercise 22.1. Does any of the information surprise you?

Exercise 22.3

Men who beat their wives often try to defend their actions by saying that their wives "drove them to it" or made them do it by yelling or screaming or bothering them. Some abusive men believe that if their wife or girlfriend hits them, it is all right for them to hit the woman. What do you think? Is there ever a time when it is acceptable for a husband to hit his wife?

Give reasons for your answer. _____

_____

_____

_____

Now take the opposite point of view. Can you think of one or more arguments to support the opposite view in this issue?

_____

_____

_____

Exercise 22.4

Work in small groups and compare your answers. Each person should give his or her opinion clearly and then give a reason or two to support that opinion.

Exercise 22.5

Read this story about a battered woman who killed her boyfriend.

> Valoree Day, a 25-year-old motel maid from Groveland, California, seemed like a "bad" battered woman. She was not passive, and, more important, she fought back when her boyfriend, Steve Brown, repeatedly assaulted her during their 16-month relationship. "My face has been permanently damaged from his beatings," says Day. Brown, a six foot one, 180-pound construction worker, was bigger and stronger than Day, who is five foot four and weighs 120 pounds. Her attempts to defend herself were therefore always unsuccessful—until Brown's final attack.
>
> On the night Brown died, according to Day, he chased her with a knife, threatened to kill her, and repeatedly stabbed at the door of the bedroom where she was hiding. When he finally caught her, he was holding his knife, and she stabbed him with a kitchen knife she had grabbed to protect herself. He bled to death.
>
> The attorneys who defended Valoree Day stated that she was only protecting herself when she stabbed her boyfriend. The prosecuting attorneys, however, disagree. They believe that Day's "violent" actions during her relationship with Brown, her not leaving the relationship, and her leaving her apartment after she stabbed Brown showed that the murder was not self-defense. The defense attorneys replied that she stayed in the relationship because she was afraid of more abuse.

Exercise 22.6

If you were the judge in this case, how would you rule? Why? Give two or three reasons to support your decision.

What do you think is an acceptable punishment—if any—for a woman who kills her abusive husband or boyfriend? Be sure to give reasons to support your answer.

Exercise 22.7

Now discuss your answers in small groups. Can you agree on what the judge should do and what the penalty should be? When you have finished, look at communication activity 37 to find out the final result of this case.

Exercise 22.8

Some people believe that women are justified in killing their batterers, but other people disagree. What is an appropriate punishment for an abusive spouse or boyfriend? Give reasons for your answer.

Do you think it matters whether the killer is a man or a woman? In other words, if a woman attacks her abusive husband or boyfriend, what should the punishment, if any, be? And if a man attacks his abusive wife or girlfriend, what should the punishment, if any, be? Does the sex of the person matter? Why or why not?

_____

_____

_____

_____

_____

_____

_____

Exercise 22.9

In small groups, discuss your responses to exercise 22.8.

Exercise 22.10

Read this situation and then answer the questions on the lines below.

In 1984, researchers in Minneapolis, Minnesota, found that violence against women could be lessened by requiring police officers to arrest abusive men when called to a home. People who agree with this idea suggest that it benefits the woman by getting the batterer out of the house and giving the woman time to look for help. People who disagree with the mandatory-arrest law fear that more violence will occur when the man returns home.

Write two or three reasons why the mandatory-arrest law would benefit battered women.

_____

_____

_____

_____

_____

_____

_____

What are two or three reasons the mandatory-arrest law would be harmful to battered women?

_____

_____

_____

_____

_____

_____

_____

Exercise 22.11

Work in small groups and discuss your answers to exercise 22.10. Do you believe that mandatory arrest would benefit or harm an abused spouse?

Exercise 22.12

Role Play

Work in small groups.

Scene: The police have been called to a house where domestic violence has occurred. To try to resolve the problem, the people involved gather in the living room for an honest discussion. Possible participants: the abusive husband (or wife), the wife (or husband), the husband's father and mother, the wife's father and mother, a police officer.

Your role:

_____

Your position on this issue:

_____

_____

_____

_____

_____

_____

_____

_____

Language Review

Read the key word or phrase (in bold) in the left column. Circle the letter of the choice that is related to the key word or phrase.

1. **batter**   a. discuss   b. participate   c. beat

2. **assault**   a. attack   b. sell   c. lock

3. **abusive**   a. useful   b. hurtful   c. independent

 4. **stalk**   a. follow   b. pile up   c. collect

 5. **prosecute**   a. let go   b. embarrass   c. bring to court

 6. **defend**   a. protect   b. damage   c. create

 7. **repeatedly**   a. once   b. again and again c. rarely

 8. **chased**   a. left   b. laughed   c. ran after

 9. **stabbed**   a. hit   b. cut with a knife c. held

10. **grabbed**   a. grew   b. held   c. showed

11. **mandatory**   a. requested   b. repeated   c. required

12. **harmful**   a. hurtful   b. amusing   c. relating to animals

13. **domestic**   a. circle   b. wildlife   c. home

14. **penalty**   a. punishment   b. reward   c. decade

15. **appeal**   a. a family   b. a decision   c. a liquid

16. **resolve**   a. a test   b. a problem   c. a small breakfast

17. **a statistic**   a. a number   b. an area   c. a problem

18. **murder**   a. kill   b. fight   c. sex

An Extreme Example of School Violence

Exercise 23.1

In 1999, an extreme case of student rebellion happened in the United States. Read this disturbing story. Then write your ideas, comments, or reactions on the lines that follow.

On April 20, 1999, high school students Dylan Klebold and Eric Harris walked into Columbine High School in Littleton, Colorado, because they wanted to kill as many people as possible. They were carrying four guns (including a 9 mm rifle) and two large bags full of different kinds of bombs. They planned to explode the bombs inside the school and then shoot any students who tried to run out.

Reports say that Klebold and Harris were members of the "Trench Coat Mafia," a group of high school students who were angry because other students treated them badly. In their yearbooks, videotapes, journals, and computer files, Klebold and Harris listed 67 people they disliked for different reasons. These reasons included students' race, religion, and high school popularity.

Reports of the attack include a story from one student who was in the school at the time: "And then one of them said, 'Get the ni——r,' [talking about an African-American student] and they shot him. It felt like a dream."

A student heard one of the gunmen shout, "This is what we always wanted to do. This is awesome (excellent)!" Yet another student saw Klebold and Harris walking in the hallway. Both were shooting guns . . . and both were laughing.

In the course of 7 1/2 minutes, the two students killed 13 people and wounded 21 before they killed themselves.

_____

_____

_____

_____

_____

_____

_____

_____

Exercise 23.2

The Columbine tragedy scared the town of Littleton, Colorado, as well as the whole country. Although people saw the attack, no one can really answer the question, "Why?" Some people say the school system and society are responsible, but many people believe the parents are responsible. In your opinion, should the parents of Dylan Klebold and Eric Harris be responsible for the horrible actions of their sons? __ Give two or three reasons for your answer.

_____

_____

_____

_____

_____

_____

_____

If you feel the parents are responsible for the attack, what punishment would you give if you were a member of the jury?

_____

_____

_____

_____

_____

Exercise 23.3

Work in small groups. Discuss your answers to and opinions about the questions in exercise 23.2.

Exercise 23.4

Read this information and then answer the questions that follow.

Some of the people of Littleton believe that the parents are responsible for their children's attack on their high school. Think about some of these facts that were discovered after the shooting.

Families of several Columbine High School victims are suing the parents of the killers and the three people who gave Harris and Klebold the guns they used to kill the students. One of their main reasons for doing this is that sheriff's officials found many bombs and guns in the students' homes.

The victims' families say the Harris and Klebold families are responsible. They believe that if the parents had watched their sons more closely, the two boys would not have been able to collect weapons and make bombs in their garages. In addition, the families say that the gunmen's parents had reason to know that their sons would use the guns to harm others. The boys had a Web site that talked about violent acts and showed anger toward and hatred of people who were different from themselves.

Has this affected your opinion about the responsibility of the parents? Why or why not? Write two or three sentences to explain your answer.

_____

_____

_____

_____

_____

_____

_____

_____

_____

_____

_____

Exercise 23.5

Work in small groups. Discuss your answers to and opinions about the question of whether the parents should be responsible for their sons' actions. What should we learn from this horrible tragedy?

Exercise 23.6

Some people say that young people are often influenced by the violence that they see on television and in video games. However, others disagree. They argue that children can understand the difference between right and wrong and that they don't copy dangerous behavior. Do young people behave violently because of television, video games, and music? Be sure to give reasons for your answer.

Exercise 23.7

Work in small groups. Discuss your answers to exercise 23.6.

Exercise 23.8

Role Play

Scene: The year is 1998, a year before the Columbine murders. At a Parent-Teacher Association meeting, people in the community are discussing the question of violence among teenagers. Possible participants: Dylan Klebold, Eric Harris, the parents of Dylan, the parents of Eric, a Columbine High student, a Columbine teacher, and a police officer.

Your role:

_____

Your position on this issue:

_____

_____

_____

_____

_____

_____

_____

 **Language Review**

Read the key word (in bold) in the left column. Circle the letter of choice that is related to the key word.

1. **kind**   a. often   b. angry   c. type

2. **journal**   a. you write it   b. you eat it   c. you visit it

3. **scared**   a. stay away from   b. afraid   c. cut

4. **horrible** a. very bad   b. very interesting c. very good

5. **rifle**   a. a big knife   b. a vegetable   c. a powerful gun

6. **explode**   a. break apart   b. come together   c. share

7. **awesome**   a. terrible   b. excellent   c. sad

8. **wounded**   a. hurt   b. laughed   c. told

9. **tragedy**   a. a happy situation   b. a terrible situation   c. a strange situation

10. **as well as**   a. and   b. but   c. perhaps

11. **sue**   a. bring to school   b. bring to work   c. bring to court

12. **weapons**   a. fork; spoon   b. gun; knife   c. brush; comb

13. **harm**   a. hurt   b. hug   c. hold

14. **several**   a. zero   b. two   c. four

Cosmetic Surgery: What Price Do We Pay for Beauty?

What is good-looking for you?

Exercise 24.1

In your opinion, what is beautiful? Read each characteristic below and show its importance by circling 1 if you think it is *very important,* 2 if you think it is *somewhat important,* 3 if you are *not sure,* 4 if you think it is *somewhat unimportant,* and 5 if you think it is *definitely unimportant.* Then write your opinion about the importance of each characteristic. Be sure to give at least one reason for your answer.

a. 1   2   3   4   5   a beautiful/handsome face

_____

_____

b. 1   2   3   4   5   a nice smile

_____

_____

c. 1   2   3   4   5   beautiful eyes

_____

_____

d. 1   2   3   4   5   a well-built (muscular) body

_____

_____

e. 1   2   3   4   5   honesty

_____

_____

f. 1   2   3   4   5   confidence

_____

_____

g. 1   2   3   4   5   a big heart

_____

_____

h. 1   2   3   4   5   a good sense of humor

_____

_____

i. 1   2   3   4   5   intelligence

_____

_____

j. 1   2   3   4   5   a tall body

_____

_____

Exercise 24.2

Work in small groups. Discuss your opinions and supporting reasons from exercise 24.1.

Exercise 24.3

If you had the choice, would you choose to be physically beautiful but unintelligent or very intelligent but physically unattractive?

_____

Write at least two reasons for your answer. _____

_____

_____

_____

_____

_____

_____

_____

Exercise 24.4

Work in small groups. Discuss your answers to exercise 24.3. Do most of the people in your group have the same answer?

Exercise 24.5

Describe your idea of a perfectly beautiful person. Circle the best adjectives.
Add your own information if necessary.

Hair:	Blond	Light Brown	Medium Brown	Dark Brown	Red
	Black	Gray	Auburn	Other: _____	

Eyes:	Hazel	Light Brown	Dark Brown	Black
	Green	Blue	Other: _____	

Height:	Short	Medium	Tall

Weight:	Skinny	Very Thin	Thin and Healthy
	A Little Heavy	Fat	Other: _____

Skin Coloring:	Light	Medium	Dark

Other: _____

Exercise 24.6

Work in small groups. Discuss your choices from exercise 24.5. Are your
answers similar to or different from the answers of the other students in your

group? _____ In what ways are they similar? _____

_____

_____

In what ways are they different? _____

_____

Do these similarities and differences surprise you? Why or why not?

_____

_____

Exercise 24.7

Read the list of things people do to make themselves more beautiful and indicate your reactions by circling 1 if you *approve strongly,* 2 if you *approve somewhat,* 3 if you *don't have a strong opinion,* 4 if you *disapprove somewhat,* and 5 if you *disapprove strongly.* Then write the reasons for your answers.

a. 1 2 3 4 5   women wearing clothes that make them look beautiful

_____

_____

b. 1 2 3 4 5   women wearing makeup

_____

_____

c. 1 2 3 4 5   men wearing makeup to help them look more attractive

_____

_____

d. 1 2 3 4 5   women wearing jewelry (rings, bracelets, earrings, necklaces)

_____

_____

e. 1   2   3   4   5   men wearing jewelry (rings, bracelets, earrings, necklaces)

_____

_____

f. 1   2   3   4   5   women having surgery to improve a physical flaw (e.g., a
                          nose operation or an operation to remove fat)

_____

_____

g. 1   2   3   4   5   men having surgery to improve a physical flaw (e.g., a
                          nose operation or a hair transplant)

_____

_____

Exercise 24.8

Work in small groups. Discuss your opinion of the behavior in exercise 24.7.

Exercise 24.9

Cosmetic surgery, surgery used to improve physical imperfections, is very popular in the world. What do you know about cosmetic surgery? Try to guess the five most common forms of cosmetic surgery from 1992 until 1998. Write your answers in the spaces provided.

1. _____

2. _____

3. _____

4. _____

5. _____

Exercise 24.10

Work with a partner and share your guesses. What guesses did your partner have that you didn't have?

_____

_____

For a list of the five most popular cosmetic procedures, see communication activity 38 after your discussion.

Exercise 24.11

Read the information about the possible benefits and risks of some cosmetic operations and then answer the questions that follow.

Benefits of Cosmetic Surgery

Face-lifts:	Remove extra skin and fat from the neck and lower half of the face. Make skin tight and remove large lines. Doctors cut the skin and remove fat.
Chemical peels:	Reduce fine lines, wrinkles, and brown spots on skin. Doctors use strong chemicals to burn away skin.
Liposuction:	Permanently remove fat from different areas of the body. Doctors make small cuts and use a machine to suck out the fat.
Breast augmentation:	Increase breast size. For breast enlargement, doctors cut the skin and insert bags of saline (saltwater) or silicone (a man-made gel).

Risks of Cosmetic Surgery

Recovery from several days to several weeks

Ugly scars   Infections   Bleeding   Death

---

a. Did you know about the risks of cosmetic surgery? _____

b. If you needed it in the future, would you have any of the above surgeries? Why or why not?

_____

_____

_____

c. Do you think physical beauty is more important than your life? Give a reason for your answer.

_____

_____

_____

Language Review

Match the vocabulary items in the left column with their definitions in the right column.

Vocabulary

___ 1. auburn

___ 2. characteristic

___ 3. cosmetic

___ 4. remove

___ 5. flaw

___ 6. hazel

___ 7. benefit

___ 8. liposuction

___ 9. reduce

___ 10. risks

___ 11. recovery

___ 12. scar

___ 13. transplant

Definition

a. permanently move something from one place to another

b. an imperfection

c. a brown-red color (usually of hair)

d. a good result from something

e. feature; trait

f. a mark left by the healing of injured tissue

g. possible problems; dangers

h. relating to beauty and physical appearance

i. the period of time after an operation when a person gets better

j. make smaller; lower in number

k. a brown-green-yellow color (usually of eyes)

l. take away; take out

m. a surgical procedure in which a doctor takes fat out of a person's body

Communication Activities

Communication Activity 1

Write this line on p. 85: "How do you know that?" I asked.

Communication Activity 2

Write this line on p. 98: "Well, the kids hate me, and the teachers hate me!"

Communication Activity 3

Mark Algren of the Applied English Center at the University of Kansas, in Lawrence, Kansas, wrote:

> The most important thing to remember is the audience. Yes, our students have to learn to adapt to being in the USA, but they get plenty of that outside our classrooms and offices. A lot of our students—and not just the ones from the Middle East—come from conservative societies. We need to remember this.
>
> My dentist does not put out magazines in his waiting room when he feels that the cover will be offensive to his patients. It might not be something that adults cannot handle, but he thinks about the children who pass through his office as well as his more conservative patients. Is he wrong to do that? I don't think so. It's good business practice if he wants to keep his patients.
>
> I don't think we need to go out of our way to be intentionally offensive under the idea of "this is the USA." If a picture is inside a magazine, students can turn the page. However, if it's on the cover, that makes it more difficult.

Communication Activity 4

Write this line on p. 17: The mother thought quietly for a minute before she answered.

Communication Activity 5

 1 across: a doctor for your teeth
 7 across: an animal that a farmer has
 8 across: a person who helps you get well
11 across: My tooth hurts. I'm going _____ the dentist's office.
14 across: This person usually wears a white uniform.
18 across: a person who helps you if you go to court
19 across: a person who works on an airplane
21 across: the person who takes care of sick animals
 1 down: the opposite of night
 3 down: I'm _____ tired! I have to sit down.
 5 down: the person who builds buildings
 9 down: I work _____ Boston Bank.
10 down: Children do this all day. They don't work.
13 down: A butcher cuts this all day.
15 down: not quick
19 down: an abbreviation for physical education class

Communication Activity 6

Write this line on p. 85: I couldn't get it down from the tree, so I called the police.

Communication Activity 7

Group 1

a. *Beauty is only skin deep.* This proverb is a little difficult to understand. It means that the beauty that a person has is only on the surface. It is only as deep as the person's skin. The real meaning is that the most important things about a person are not the person's physical appearance but rather the person's personality and other individual characteristics. These things are much deeper than the skin because they are "deep" inside the person.

b. *It is better to give than to receive.* The proverb is not so difficult to understand. It means that it is better to give things to people than to receive things from people. It means that you will feel better if you give something to someone than if you receive something from someone.

Communication Activity 8

You are an animal rights activist. You believe that animal life is equal to human life. It's not good for a human to suffer, but it's not good for an animal to suffer either.

Communication Activity 9

Write this line on p. 98: "Well, number one, you're 52 years old. Number two, you're the principal!"

Communication Activity 10

 1 across: What do people fly on?
 5 across: I am going _____ France.
 6 across: a large city in Canada
 8 across: What do you see in a museum?
11 across: _____ York
15 across: Today I run; yesterday I _____.
17 across: money for the government
19 across: a small body of water
21 across: on an airplane: a window seat or an _____ seat
 1 down: a country in Europe
 3 down: A U.S. passport is _____ orange.
 4 down: ten minus eight
 9 down: _____ do; do again
10 down: the same as #4 down
13 down: I went to England _____ 1995.
14 down: a house for when you are camping
18 down: eggs, cheese, meat, bread

Communication Activity 11

Write this line on p. 85: When he said this, I was very upset. "Please!" I said. "Please come get my cat!"

Communication Activity 12

Write this line on p. 17: One day a little girl was standing in the kitchen.

Communication Activity 13

The result: The dog was not killed.

The real story: Taro was a 115-pound Akita that "scratched" the owner's niece over the holidays. There were no formal complaints, but when the police heard about it, they entered the picture. The girl was not seriously hurt, and it was a family matter. If Taro had been a vicious dog, the little girl would have been killed. After much controversy, then-governor Christine Whitman released Taro as property to his owner, but she said that the dog could no longer live in the state of New Jersey. Despite predictions of more Taro terror to come, the dog lived out the rest of his uneventful life in upstate New York and died peacefully several years ago. Assemblyman Azzolina, who introduced the first law, later revised the law to prevent other dogs from being accused.

Communication Activity 14

Here is the whole story: Mila Bertelli lived in an old multistory condominium in a beach resort area in Italy. Most of the other owners did not live in the build-ing. They only came in summertime. It was winter, so she was by herself for the whole weekend. On Friday evening, she took the elevator downstairs to buy a newspaper and some cigarettes. When she was coming back up in the elevator, it got stuck. There was no guard on duty downstairs that weekend, and there was no emergency phone in the old elevator, so she had to stay in the elevator Friday night, all day Saturday, and all day Sunday. On Monday morning, when the guard came back, he noticed that the elevator was not working and called for help. Mila had only a newspaper and a pack of cigarettes. She did not have any matches. The elevator had lights, so she was able to read the paper while she was waiting for help to arrive on Monday morning.

Communication Activity 15

The U.S. Postal Service had to choose between a correct version of history and its tight budget. In the end, the agency decided that it could not allow the mis-take to remain. A new sheet of stamps with the correct picture of Bill Pickett was printed.

Communication Activity 16

Write this line on p. 85: One day I was playing with my sister's cat, and it ran outside.

Communication Activity 17

Write this line on p. 98: "Wake up, son. It's time to go to school."

Communication Activity 18

Shannon Faulkner was a student at the Citadel for only one week. After a week of training, she dropped out of the school without saying why she did this. She continued to fight her case that women should be permitted to enter the school. In 1995, the Supreme Court decided not to make a decision on this case because Faulkner was no longer at the school. Therefore, there was not any decision about the Citadel and female students.

The real test came a year later at a similar school, the Virginia Military Institute (VMI), which was also a male-only school. VMI wanted to avoid a similar situation, so it created a similar program for female students. Female students challenged this "similar" program in court. The courts decided that the creation of the similar program for female students by the state of Virginia and VMI was fair.

However, in 1996, the Supreme Court threw out all lower court decisions and said that the similar program was not equal education. If VMI wanted to continue to receive the millions of dollars that it received every year in federal government money, it would have to open its doors to all students, both male and female. The only way for VMI to continue to accept only male students was to change to a private school, which would have been extremely expensive at approximately $337 million dollars.

In September 1996, the board of VMI voted nine to eight to allow women on the campus starting in the fall of 1997. This ended the 157-year-old tradition of accepting only male students.

Female students were very happy about the news, but not everyone shared their joy. Robert Patterson, who was the chief lawyer for the effort to keep female students out of the school and who graduated from VMI in 1943, said, "It's a sad day for VMI. It's a sad day for the state, and it's a sad day for the nation as far as I'm concerned."

Communication Activity 19

You are a veterinarian. You love animals. You have worked with animals all your life. You have tried hard to save their lives.

Communication Activity 20

Write this line on p. 17: The little girl thought for a minute, and then she asked, "Well, Mom, why are all of Grandma's hairs white?"

Communication Activity 21

Write this line on p. 85: The man answered, "Have you ever seen a dead cat in a tree?"

Communication Activity 22

When the case went to court, the decision was in favor of Mrs. Alston. The court said that Mrs. Alston had a right to some of the Lotto money. Mr. Alston was not happy with this decision, and he used his legal right to appeal (protest) this decision to a higher court. The circuit court (regional court) listened to both sides of this case. In the end, the seven judges voted 6-1 in favor of Mr. Alston. The judges gave two reasons for their decision. First, Mr. Alston used his own money to buy the Lotto ticket. The second reason is related to the first reason. The judges said that in this case, one person did not help the other person get the Lotto ticket in any way. Therefore, the money was Mr. Alston's. The decision of the judges was not unanimous (6-1), but almost all of the judges agreed with Mr. Alston's side of the situation.

Communication Activity 23

Group 2

a. *Do unto others as you would like them to do unto you.* This proverb means that you should treat people in the same way that you want them to treat you. If you don't want people to gossip about you, then don't gossip about anyone. If you want someone to say nice things about the way you look today, then say nice things about the way other people look. You should do things to people that you want them to do to you.

b. *If you want to keep a friend, never borrow, never lend.* Some people think that it is not a good thing to mix friendship with business or money. If you borrow from a friend or lend something to a friend, this might cause problems. What if you can't return the money that you have borrowed? You might lose a friend. Therefore, in order to keep a friend, it's best not to borrow anything from that friend or lend anything to that friend.

Communication Activity 24

Write this line on p. 98: "Give me two reasons why you don't want to go to school."

Communication Activity 25

Several states, including Illinois, have recently made new laws that allow parents of students who miss school too many times to be put in jail. For example, in Springfield, Illinois, six mothers were charged with a misdemeanor because their children were repeatedly absent from school. These parents did not go to jail, but the new law in Illinois allows police to arrest parents if their children miss school too often. School and state officials believe that this is a good solution to the problem of excessive student absence.

Communication Activity 26

Write this line on p. 85: After I looked for the cat, I found it very high up in a tree.

Communication Activity 27

  1 across: If your tooth hurts, you might ask this person for help.
  4 across: you and I
  8 across: a person you visit when you are sick
10 across: a student uses this
14 across: a person who takes care of you when you are sick
16 across: It sounds just like the number eight.
19 across: the person who flies an airplane for a profession
20 across: The child said, "I want to _____ a doctor when I grow up."
  1 down: Some people work at night, but most people work during the _____.
  2 down: This person works in a classroom.
  5 down: the person who plans and builds buildings
  6 down: When I grow _____, I want to be a teacher.
10 down: What do children do all day? They don't work.
12 down: The company is_____ the second floor of this building.
15 down: the opposite of fast
17 down: Sometimes a teacher gives a _____ to students.

Communication Activity 28

Write this line on p. 17: She was watching her mother wash the dishes.

Communication Activity 29

Michele Bowman of the Haggerty Intensive English Language Program at SUNY (State University of New York—New Paltz) wrote:

> I teach at an intensive English program where we also make some magazines and newspapers available to our students. Personally, I am against any type of censorship. The magazines that we make available are not pornographic and are regular news and entertainment magazines that are acceptable in U.S. society. If the students are in the U.S., they should get accustomed to, or at least be aware of this type of representation in the media.
>
> How do you have the magazines displayed? We have a large library type of magazine shelf where the magazines can be overlapped but are standing upright. If there are some magazines that you think might embarrass some students, place them under another magazine. Perhaps the most important point here is that none of the students has complained to you about this. If no one has said anything, maybe the best thing is to leave it alone.

Communication Activity 30

You are a medical scientist. You have done a lot of research. You believe that using animals is the only way to find a real cure for this horrible disease. You know that using computers or other ways will not work because AIDS is such a difficult disease.

Communication Activity 31

Write this line on p. 85: The man at the police department told me that police officers do not help cats.

Communication Activity 32

Write this line on p. 98: "Give me two reasons why I should go to school."

Communication Activity 33

   1 across: Where does a flight attendant work?
   4 across: to go around a place to see it
   6 across: This city in Canada starts with the letter *t*.
  11 across: the opposite of old
  12 across: My _____ from Miami to London was late.
  17 across: the extra money you pay to the government
  18 across: It is _____ to go to a party.
  20 across: blue or green
   1 down: Warsaw is the capital of _____.
   2 down: We stayed _____ home.
   4 down: one, _____, three
   7 down: When we aren't working, we can do this.
  10 down: six minus four
  12 down: Paris is in _____.
  14 down: a temporary house made of cloth
  16 down: a car that you use for a short ride

Communication Activity 34

Group 3
a. *First impressions are the most lasting.* The first impression that a person makes on you is the strongest impression. It is the impression that you will keep in your mind for a long time. It is the most important one because you will continue to think of that person in a certain way because of the first impression that you had. It's important to make a good impression from the very beginning because first impressions will last the longest time.
b. *It's better to be safe than sorry.* This proverb means that it is better to take an extra step to be sure about something than it is to take a chance that you might do something wrong.

Communication Activity 35

Write this line on p. 17: She said, "Well, every time you do something wrong and make me angry or make me cry, one of my hairs turns white."

Communication Activity 36

Write this line on p. 85: "Sir, we can't do that. But it's okay. The cat will come down when it is hungry."

Communication Activity 37

A judge convicted Valoree Day of involuntary manslaughter (killing someone, usually by accident) and sentenced her to six years in prison. She later appealed the judge's decision. She said that her first attorney didn't explain enough about the experiences of battered women. The new judge decided to allow Day to return to court to defend herself again.

Communication Activity 38

The five most common are liposuction, breast augmentation, eyelid surgery, face-lifts, and chemical peels.

Communication Activity 39

Write this line on p. 98: Early one morning a mother went into her son's room to wake him up.

Communication Activity 40

You are a medical doctor. You have worked all your life with human beings. You have tried hard to save their lives.

Communication Activity 41

Write this line on p. 85 The next day the cat came home and ate breakfast.

Communication Activity 42

The case was decided by a jury. The jury found that McCummings should receive the money because the policeman should not have fired a gun since there was no probable cause to believe that McCummings was going to use deadly force. He was in fact running away at the time.

    The New York City Transit Authority appealed the decision. The New York State Court of Appeals found that it could not reverse the decision. The court said that it "could not avoid what may seem to some to be an unacceptable resolution of the factual disputes." The court agreed that the Transit Authority had to pay McCummings 4.3 million dollars.

The Transit Authority was still not satisfied and appealed the case to the U.S. Supreme Court. However, the Supreme Court agreed with the lower courts' decisions and ordered the Transit Authority to pay the $4.3 million.

Communication Activity 43

The term *three hots and a cot* literally means three hot meals and a place to sleep. This term is often used by people who either are not unhappy when they are arrested or purposely try to get into prison because they are more comfortable in prison than they are on the streets due specifically to their poor living conditions.

Communication Activity 44

Write this line on p. 17: She asked, "Why are some of your hairs white, Mom?"

Communication Activity 45

Write this line on p. 98: "Oh, you can't stay home just because the teachers and the students hate you."

Communication Activity 46

Write this line on p. 85: The cat didn't return the next day, so I looked for it.

Communication Activity 47

Group 4
a. *There is no time like the present.* This proverb means that you should not wait to do things until tomorrow or the next day. It means that the best time to do something is usually now.
b. *If you lie down with dogs, you will get up with fleas.* A flea is a small insect that bites dogs. We associate fleas with dogs; it is a natural combination. If you sleep with dogs, you will have fleas. This proverb means that if you hang around with people who behave badly, you will catch some of those bad characteristics.

Communication Activity 48

You are an AIDS patient. You are taking medicine for AIDS, but you have many health problems. Your doctor is worried that the medicine may stop working. You believe that using animals is the only way to find a real cure for this horrible disease.

Communication Activity 49

The school decided that one of the magazines seemed to have more material that possibly could be offensive to some students, so the school stopped receiving and displaying that magazine. There is of course occasional nudity in some of the other magazines, but the school officials report that this seems to be a nonissue these days. In any case, the school never received a single complaint from any student about any of the magazines.

Communication Activity 50

Here is the whole story: Thieves stole the Wheelers' driveway, the place in front of the house where they park their car. The driveway was made of gravel (small rocks), and the thieves dug up the gravel and took it away.

Communication Activity 51

Write this line on p. 98: "But Mom, I don't want to go to school!"

Communication Activity 52

Write this line on p. 17: The little girl saw that her mother had a few white hairs in her brown hair.

Communication Activity 53

4 across: a trip to a place
5 across: I am going _____ the store.
8 across: Paintings and sculptures are sometimes called _____.
12 across: What is your _____ number?
15 across: I _____ back to my apartment because I forgot my book.
18 across: If people have _____, they laugh.
19 across: San Francisco _____

20 across: yellow or purple
21 across: the area between sections of seats in an airplane
 2 down: We stayed _____ the Hilton Hotel.
 3 down: Paris is _____ in China.
 7 down: not work
 9 down: His work was wrong, so he had to _____ do it.
12 down: People in _____ speak French.
13 down: I put it _____ my pocket.
16 down: a cab
18 down: fruit, vegetables, spaghetti

Communication Activity 54

 4 across: my cousin and I
 7 across: an animal on a farm
10 across: a teacher uses this
11 across: The student is walking _____ school now.
16 across: It rhymes with <u>gate.</u>
18 across: a person who helps you with legal problems
20 across: The teacher said, "I want to _____ sure my students understand this."
21 across: a doctor for animals
 2 down: This person works in a school.
 3 down: I'm _____ hungry! I have to eat now.
 6 down: the opposite of down
 9 down: I study _____ the library.
12 down: The book is _____ the shelf.
13 down: What does a butcher sell?
17 down: a way for a teacher to find out what students have learned
19 down: A teacher who teaches sports is sometimes called a _____ teacher.

Communication Activity 55

Group 5
a. *Don't wash your dirty linen in public.* The phrase *dirty linen* does not refer to dirty sheets here. It represents secret things or private things about you or your family. This proverb means that it is not good to talk about your personal problems in public.
b. *There are plenty of other fish in the sea.* This proverb is not talking about fish! It means that there are many people in the world. It means that the per-

son that you wanted is not available but there are many other good people available.

Communication Activity 56

Baseball commissioner Bud Selig suspended John Rocker for the first month of the baseball season, required him to pay a fine, and ordered him to go to sensitivity training, saying that John Rocker had "brought dishonor to himself, his team, and major league baseball." Ted Turner, the owner of the Atlanta Braves, said that Rocker deserved another chance because he had apologized to those he had offended. Some time later, however, Rocker was traded to another team.

Communication Activity 57

1. b. a horse 2. a. a bird 3. b. a chicken 4. a. cat 5. a. an elephant 6. c. a wolf 7. b. a lion 8. c. an owl 9. a. a dog 10. a. a monkey

Communication Activity 58

1. cats, dogs 2. wolf, sheep's 3. cat 4. horse 5. snake 6. monkeying (*or* horsing) 7. horsing (*or* monkeying) 8. frog 9. butterflies 10. ants

Communication Activity 59

The show was controversial, but it was allowed to continue as planned.

Answer Key

Unit 1

Language Review, p. 6: 1. passed   2. breed   3. restrain   4. wound
5. guilty   6. sentenced   7. activist   8. lenient   9. vicious   10. treat
11. public   12. described   13. bit   14. let   15. ridiculous   16. niece
17. true   18. became   19. lip   20. owner

Unit 2

Language Review, p. 14: 1. b   2. b   3. a   4. a   5. b   6. c   7. a   8. c
9. b   10. a   11. b   12. b   13. b   14. a   15. b   16. b   17. b   18. b
19. a   20. b   21. a   22. a   23. c   24. b   25. c

Unit 3

Language Review, p. 18: 1. c   2. a   3. d   4. e   5. b   6. i   7. l   8. f
9. k   10. j   11. g   12. h

Unit 4

Crossword puzzle, p. 20:
Language Review, p. 21: 1. c   2. a   3. a
4. c   5. b   6. b   7. a   8. b   9. a
10. c   11. b   12. a   13. a   14. c   15. b
16. c   17. b   18. b   19. a   20. b

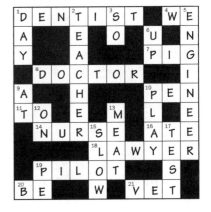

Unit 5

Language Review, p. 28: 1. b   2. a   3. c
4. b   5. a   6. a   7. b   8. b   9. c
10. a   11. c   12. a   13. a   14. b   15. b
16. a   17. a   18. c   19. a   20. b   21. b
22. c

Unit 6

Language Review, p. 37: 1. c   2. a   3. b   4. a   5. a   6. c   7. b   8. c
9. a   10. b   11. c   12. c   13. a   14. a   15. c

Unit 7
Language Review, p. 41: 1. c   2. g   3. d   4. i   5. k   6. m   7. l   8. a
9. f   10. j   11. e   12. h   13. b   14. o   15. n   16. p

Unit 8
Language Review, p. 44: 1. b   2. f   3. d   4. h   5. i   6. e   7. j   8. a
9. g   10. c   11. l   12. k

Unit 9
Language Review, p. 48: 1. a   2. b   3. a   4. b   5. a   6. b   7. c   8. c
9. a   10. b   11. b   12. a

Unit 10
Language Review, p. 59: Part a: 1. b   2. d   3. g   4. f   5. h   6. c   7. a   8. e
Part b: 1. c   2. e   3. f   4. a   5. h   6. g   7. d   8. b

Unit 11
Language Review, p. 62: 1. b   2. a   3. a   4. a   5. c   6. a   7. c   8. c
9. c   10. b

Unit 12
Language Review, p. 70: 1. b   2. a   3. a   4. a   5. b   6. c   7. a   8. b
9. c   10. c

Unit 13
Language Review, p. 74: 1. b   2. a   3. b   4. b   5. b   6. a   7. b   8. c
9. c   10. b   11. a   12. c   13. c   14. b   15. c   16. a   17. b   18. b
19. b   20. a

Unit 14
Language Review, p. 82: 1. b   2. a   3. c   4. a   5. a   6. b   7. c   8. b
9. a   10. c   11. b   12. b   13. c   14. a   15. c   16. b   17. b   18. a
19. a   20. b

Unit 15
Language Review, p. 86: 1. c   2. d   3. a   4. e   5. b   6. i   7. j   8. h
9. f   10. g

Unit 16
Crossword puzzle, p. 88:
Language Review, p. 89: 1. a   2. b   3. c
4. a   5. b   6. c   7. c   8. a   9. a
10. c   11. a   12. c   13. c   14. a   15. b
16. a   17. a   18. a

Unit 17
Language Review, p. 96: Part a: 1. b   2. d
3. f   4. e   5. c   6. a   7. g   8. h   9. i
10. j   Part b: 1. c   2. d   3. f   4. b   5. a
6. e   7. j   8. g   9. h   10. i

Unit 18
Language Review, p. 100: 1. b   2. d   3. a   4. c   5. e   6. f   7. j   8. h
9. i   10. g

Unit 19
Language Review, p. 105: 1. b   2. a   3. b   4. a   5. b   6. a   7. a   8. a
9. b   10. a   11. b   12. b   13. a   14. b   15. b   16. a   17. a   18. a
19. b   20. a   21. a   22. b

Unit 20
Language Review, p. 111: Part a: 1. b   2. d   3. f   4. h   5. c   6. g   7. a   8. e
Part b: 1. c   2. i   3. e   4. f   5. g   6. b   7. h   8. a   9. d

Unit 21
Language Review, p. 119: Part a: 1. b   2. e   3. h   4. f   5. i   6. g   7. d
8. a   9. c   Part b: 1. b   2. a   3. g   4. f   5. d   6. e   7. c

Unit 22
Language Review, p. 126: 1. c   2. a   3. b   4. a   5. c   6. a   7. b   8. c
9. b   10. b   11. c   12. a   13. c   14. a   15. b   16. b   17. a   18. a

Unit 23
Language Review, p. 133: 1. c   2. a   3. b   4. a   5. c   6. a   7. b   8. a
9. b   10. a   11. c   12. b   13. a   14. c

Unit 24
Language Review, p. 143: 1. c   2. e   3. h   4. l   5. b   6. k   7. d   8. m
9. j   10. g   11. i   12. f   13. a